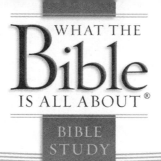

WHAT THE
Bible
IS ALL ABOUT®

BIBLE
STUDY
SERIES

The Life of
Jesus

MATTHEW THROUGH JOHN

His Life, Death, Resurrection and Ministry

Based on *What the Bible Is All About* by Dr. Henrietta C. Mears

Written by Bayard Taylor, M.Div.
Dr. Gary S. Greig, Editorial Director for Bible and Theology

Gospel Light
The Bible. Pure and Simple.

D1089278

Published by Regal
From Gospel Light
Ventura, California, U.S.A.
www.regalbooks.com
Printed in the U.S.A.

Rights for publishing this book outside the U.S.A. or in non-English languages are administered by Gospel Light Worldwide, an international not-for-profit ministry. For additional information, please visit www.glww.org, email info@glww.org, or write to Gospel Light Worldwide, 1957 Eastman Avenue, Ventura, CA 93003, U.S.A.

To order copies of this book and other Regal products in bulk quantities, please contact us at 1-800-446-7735.

CONTENTS

HOW TO USE THIS STUDY

In *The Life of Jesus*, based on Dr. Henrietta Mears's *What the Bible Is All About*, you will study the four accounts of Jesus' life and ministry as recorded in the books of Matthew, Mark, Luke and John. During the 12 sessions of study in this book, you will get a better understanding of the key events in Jesus' life—His miraculous birth, His ministry, His teachings, and His crucifixion and resurrection—and see how each Gospel evangelist chose to emphasize particular themes.

Each session begins with an overview of the material that includes the following:

- **Session Focus:** Explains the main theme of the portion of the Bible being examined.

- **Key Verses to Memorize:** Important passages of Scripture that you may want to commit to heart. As Joshua 1:8 states, "Keep this Book of the Law always on your lips; meditate on it day and night, so that you may be careful to do everything written in it. Then you will be prosperous and successful."

- **Weekly Reading:** A listing of the chapters in the Bible that will be covered during the session and a suggested breakdown for how to read the material during a five-day period.

- **Session at a Glance:** Provides an outline for leaders on how to structure the material in a group setting (both 60-minute and 90-minute options are provided).

Before beginning each session, it is recommended that you read the portions of Scripture listed in the weekly reading section of the overview. At the end of each session, you will find a number of personal application and study questions based on these chapters in the Bible and on the background material presented in that session's reading. These questions have been written to allow you to reflect on the material and apply the ideas presented in the session to your life. You can answer these questions individually or incorporate them as part of a small-group discussion.

READING THE BIBLE AS IT WAS MEANT TO BE READ

Dr. Henrietta C. Mears

Dr. Henrietta C. Mears was the director of Christian Education at Hollywood Presbyterian Church for many years and the founder of Gospel Light Publications, Gospel Light Worldwide, and the Forest Home Christian Conference Center in the San Bernardino Mountains of California. In this capacity, Mears put together a highly successful three-year high school curriculum on the whole Bible, which serves as the foundation for this study guide series.

Mears was a modern-day champion of the "Christo-centric" interpretation of the Bible, whereby Christ is considered to be the center of all the themes of both the Old and New Testaments. At a time when others were centered on historicism, the evolution of the idea of monotheism, genre studies or the study of the communities out of which certain writings were presumed to arise, Henrietta steadfastly kept the focus on Jesus. In this persistent attention to the centrality of Jesus Christ, Henrietta was in good company: This same impulse has been found in the best thinkers of the Church throughout the centuries—including Augustine, Basil the Great and John Chrysostom—and it had its start in the Bible itself.

The following is an original article by Dr. Henrietta C. Mears titled "The Bible: Christo-centric." Read it carefully—it packs a lot of punch![1]

The Bible: Christo-centric

There is one principal subject of the Bible to which every other subject is related. The Bible is Christo-centric. Take Christ out of the Old Testament and the whole structure falls apart. The Book, from Genesis to Revelation, has but one theme—*the Bible speaks only of Jesus Christ.* You remember Paul said to the Corinthians, "I determined not to know any thing among you, save Jesus Christ, and Him crucified" (1 Corinthians 2:2). That is the theme of the Bible from beginning to end.

The Key that Unlocks

The subject of the Old Testament is the same as the New. Each complements the other. Neither is complete without the other. They both are "the witness that God has borne concerning His Son" (1 John 5:9, *ASV*). No one can ever understand the Bible unless he sees Christ on every page.[2] He is the One who solves the difficulties in interpretation. He is the key that unlocks every page.

There is a story told of some knights coming to an old castle. The gate was closed and locked. How they wished they could get within the walls, but they could not climb over them. They found a bunch of keys, and eagerly tried each one. How they worked and struggled, but the gate did not respond. Finally, they put in one of the keys, and the great lock came open without the slightest difficulty. Do you suppose those men doubted for a moment that they had found the right key?

This old story reminds us of men going to the Bible. It seems like a Book of Mystery to them. They have tried every key to open it, but every key has failed. The key of man's wisdom has been tried to unlock its treasures, but without success. There is, however, one key that even the humblest can put into the lock, and with Him the gate of understanding opens. Shall we doubt then that Christ is the right key? He is more than the key. He says, "I am the Way, and the Truth" (John 14:6).

The Picture that Reveals

Two little boys were trying to put a puzzle map together. It was a map of the United States. After they had been struggling awhile, one of the little fellows said, "I don't know what a country looks like, but I do know what a man looks like." And so with that they turned it on the other side and with ease put together the face of Abraham Lincoln. It was not hard for them to find where the eye, the ear, the mouth and the forehead went. After it was completed, they turned it over and what do you suppose they found? Yes, the map of the United States.

If you can only find the picture of Christ in the Bible, you will find that the things which seem to puzzle you fit in perfect harmony with the whole. Christ said on one occasion, "Search the Scriptures; for in them ye think ye have eternal life: and they are they which testify of Me" (John 5:39). If we do not find Christ when we study the Scriptures, we study in vain.

ALL TEXTS LEAD TO CHRIST

An old and great minister of the gospel listened to a young minister preach one day. After the sermon the young man, wishing to have the criticism of this experienced older man, asked him what he thought of his sermon.

"Well, now that you ask me, I must tell you that I find one serious fault. There was no Christ in your sermon."

"But," said the young man, "there was no Christ in my text."

"Well," said the elder, "where did you find it?"

"I found it in the Bible, of course."

"Ah," said the old warrior of the faith, "you cannot find a text in the Bible in which there is no Christ. Do you not know, young man, that in England all roads lead to London? And in the Bible every passage points to Calvary?"

"But I do not quite see the way," said the young man.

To this the older man replied, "Then you must find the way, and if you cannot find the way jump over hedges and ditches; but get to Jesus somehow."

A SINGLE THEME

This really is the wonder of the Bible—that it has but one theme and that theme is the Lord Jesus Christ.

If this is so, and Jesus is the subject of the Book, where should we begin? We want to learn all we possibly can about the Lord Jesus Christ, and how shall we commence the study in order that we may? Shall we begin with Genesis and go right through the Book? Some think that if Christ is the main theme of the Bible then we should begin with the Gospels, for they portray His birth, His death and His resurrection. But Matthew begins by saying, "The book of the generation of Jesus Christ, the son of David, the son of Abraham" (Matthew 1:1) He sends you right back to the Old Testament.

Luke goes back further than Matthew, and in giving the genealogy of Jesus Christ he says, "Which was the son of Seth, which was the son of Adam, which was the son of God" (Luke 3:38).

John begins by saying, "In the beginning was the Word, and the Word was with God, and the Word was God" (John 1:1).

Each one of the Gospels takes us back into the Old Testament. Once we know who Christ is from the Gospels, we can go back to the Old Testament and with intelligence and understanding trace His coming into the world. Remember, when Jesus was talking to the men on the way to Emmaus, He began "at Moses and all the prophets," and "expounded unto them in all the scriptures the things concerning Himself" (Luke 24:27).

If we open a novel in the middle and begin to read about the hero, we will soon find that we will have to go back to the beginning and start the book where we should if we are to understand the story, otherwise the plot will be veiled to us. John says, "In the beginning was the Word, and the Word was with God"; then he adds, "all things were made by Him; and without Him was not any thing made that was made" (John 1:1-2). When I turn back to the verse of the first book of the Bible, I read, "In the beginning GOD" (Genesis 1:1), and we see the Creator God who was the Word. We find Jesus in the beginning and all through the book of Genesis.

A VERY INTERESTING THING IS THIS

When you study the Gospels and Acts, in fact any of the Scriptures, you find that the plan of redemption was no afterthought, but it was a clear unfolding of the eternal purpose of God. We read words like this: "The Lamb slain from the foundation of the world" (Revelation 13:8). Can we find anything of this purpose in the Old Testament? If God has a definite idea in mind by which He is to redeem mankind, we cannot help but find Him revealing that purpose. We will see examples in the Old Testament of God working out that principle. Then when the fulness of time was come, God sent His Son into the world to reveal His plan.

We know that it was God's plan to save the world by having His own Son come down to this earth and take upon Himself the form of a man. We call this "the incarnation." This comes from the Latin *in* (meaning "in") and *caro* (meaning "flesh"). Webster says, "the union of Godhead with manhood." God's plan was not to redeem men by giving them a set of rules or by establishing a philosophy of life, but by coming down and being made flesh and living among us.

If it was God's plan to save the world by a personality and that Person was to be His Son, we may expect to see Him puttting His plan in operation from the very beginning of His revelation in the Scriptures. This is just what God does. One of the most interesting and illuminating of all of the studies in the Old Testament is to trace the ancestral line of the Messiah. God reveals everything through His Son. It begins with a promise in Genesis 3:15: "And I will put enmity between thee and the woman, and between thy seed and her seed; it shall bruise thy head, and thou shalt bruise his heel."

Sin Demands a Saviour

It is the fall in the Garden of Eden that makes a Saviour necessary. The fallen race must be lifted up and restored to God. "As in Adam all die, even so in Christ shall all be made alive" (1 Corinthians 15:22). "For as by one man's disobedience many were made sinners, so by the obedience of one shall many be made righteous" (Romans 5:19).

> Love lifted me!
> Love lifted me!
> When nothing else could help,
> Love lifted me!

Christ says that He came to "destroy the works of the devil" (1 John 3:8). It was at the very moment man sinned that God announced His gracious purpose to redeem the world. It is from this promise of the "seed of the woman" that we see the whole plan of God concerning a Saviour unfolding before us. This "seed of woman" (not of man, as in the case of all other men), who was none other than Jesus Christ, should come into the world following a very definite order of events. This is not at all strange, for history rightly interpreted is simply His Story. All history is related to the Lord Jesus Christ, and without human design, all history is dated from His advent into the world; it is either BC or AD.

Christ a Member of Our Race

Through the long centuries, God's plan of redemption is expanding from stage to stage. Someone has said that if it were left to man to conceive of a method of redemption, he would have thought of some celestial being, but God says the Saviour of the world is to be "the seed of the woman." This prophetic statement in Genesis 3:15 does not tell us anything about the nature of His person or work, but these are to appear step by step throughout the coming centuries. We know that He will be a member of our race. "Therefore the Lord Himself shall give you a sign; Behold, a virgin shall conceive, and bear a son, and shall call His name Immanuel" (Isaiah 7:14).

THE STORY OF THE GREATEST HERO

The story of the life of any hero is always fascinating. The Bible relates the most thrilling stories of all literature, and they all lead up to the greatest of all heroes, Jesus Christ. When once you have learned something of the theme of the Bible, which is Jesus Christ, first in the New Testament and discover something of His work and character, then when you go back to the Old Testament, you see Him throwing light on every passage. He will take you by the hand and walk with you all through the Old Testament, as He did those two men on the way to Emmaus, and finally lead you back to the New Testament. Then you will find that it is the very same Jesus who all the prophets had said would come.

Remember, all through this study of the bloodline of the King, that Christ is the center and fulfillment of the promise of "the seed of the woman" from the first man Adam until Jesus is born in Bethlehem, when the fulness of time was come. In Christ's veins ran the royal blood of many great individuals. Of the great number of names given in the genealogy of Jesus Christ, seven are outstanding. Commit these names to your memory in their proper order, and it will give you an outline of the Bible that deals with the 4,000 years of messianic history: Adam, Shem, Abraham, Isaac, Jacob, Judah and David.

The Messiah was to come. God had promised Him. Over and over again He makes a fresh statement of this promise to individuals. The prophets spoke of His coming, and every Jew expected a Messiah. All of these promises and predictions were fulfilled in Christ, the Son of God.

Notes

1. Originally published in *Highlights of Scripture Part One: (A) Through the Bible By Periods and (B) The Blood Line of the Messiah* (Los Angeles, CA: The Gospel Light Press, 1937), pp. 55-61. Note that Dr. Mears used the British spelling for "Saviour" and the masculine pronoun "he" to refer to both men and women. She also apparently quoted Bible passages from memory, and not always word for word. We have added Scripture references where she did not include the verse.
2. Perhaps a bit of hyperbole. Some pages are full of genealogies, and some are tales of woe brought on by sin. The point is that Christ is the main subject of the Bible from the beginning to the end.

JESUS, THE WORD
Christ's Presence in the Beginning (John 1)

SESSION FOCUS
God the Son, Jesus Christ, was present from the time of creation.

KEY VERSE TO MEMORIZE
In the beginning was the Word, and the Word was
with God, and the Word was God.
JOHN 1:1

WEEKLY READING

DAY 1	John 1; Genesis 1
DAY 2	Psalm 19; Colossians 1
DAY 3	Colossians 2; Philippians 2
DAY 4	Hebrews 1–2
DAY 5	Hebrews 3–4

FOR LEADERS: SESSION AT A GLANCE

SESSION OUTLINE	60 MIN.	90 MIN.	WHAT YOU WILL DO
Getting started	10	15	Pray and worship
Main points of the chapter	25	35	Discuss how Jesus is God's Word to us
Application and discussion	15	25	Discuss personal application questions
Looking ahead	5	5	Prepare for next week
Wrapping up	5	10	Close with prayer or song

Works and Words

When Jesus was on this earth, He performed many miracles and told many parables. We could also call these Jesus' works and words, or His deeds and declarations. In each case, notice what comes first: *action*. The gospel is not just talk; it's about living out the truth in real life. It is about God intervening in concrete human experience.

Yet the gospel cannot be reduced merely to actions. Words are important. The fact that Jesus fulfilled prophecy needs explanation! Jesus' preferred method of teaching was through storytelling (or parables). The Church's proclamation of the gospel expressed God's actions and God's wisdom in authoritative declarations. Jesus is the Word that supports all truthful words.

THE GOSPELS AND THE GOSPEL

Our primary written sources for the life of Jesus Christ come from four books, which, according to early Christian tradition, were written by early followers of Jesus. These books are as follows:

1. The Gospel According to Matthew: Although this Gospel does not name its author, by the end of the second century it had generally been ascribed to Matthew, a former tax collector and one of the original 12 disciples. This tradition can be traced to Papias of Hierapolis (c. AD 125–150), who wrote that "Matthew put together the sayings [of Jesus] in the Hebrew dialect."[1]

2. The Gospel According to Mark: This Gospel also does not name its author, but an early tradition preserved by Eusebius ascribed it to Mark the Evangelist (also known as John Mark), who was a disciple of Peter and cousin of Barnabas (see Colossians 4:10).

3. The Gospel According to Luke: The Early Church Fathers Jerome and Eusebius ascribed the authorship of this Gospel to Luke, a doctor who accompanied the apostle Paul on his missionary journey (see Colossians 4:14). The book appears to have been written for a person named Theophilus (see Luke 1:1-4), though scholars are unsure if this refers to an actual person or is just an honorary title (the name means "friend of

God"). Luke also wrote the book of Acts for this individual (see Acts 1:1-2).

4. The Gospel According to John: The author of this Gospel identifies himself only as the "disciple whom Jesus loved" (John 21:7), but by the beginning of the second century AD it had generally been ascribed to John, one of Jesus' original 12 disciples and a member of his "inner circle" of three (along with Peter and James; see Matthew 17:1).

The word "gospel" itself (Greek *euangelion*) simply means "good news." When it is capitalized, it always refers to the books of Matthew, Mark, Luke and John. When it is lowercased, it refers to the message about Jesus' death on the cross and His victory over the grave. The Gospels preserve and announce the gospel. The gospel is not just "good" news—it is the best news ever!

The Synoptic Gospels

The books of Matthew, Mark and Luke are called the Synoptic Gospels because they synchronize fairly closely with each other in chronology and content. Many scholars believe they were written before AD 70, the fateful year the Roman legions under the emperor Titus destroyed Jerusalem and Jerusalem's Temple.[2]

Each of the Gospel writers had his own particular point of view and wrote for a specific audience. Matthew, writing to a Jewish audience, demonstrated throughout his Gospel how Jesus was the fulfillment of the Hebrew Bible's prophecies of the promised Messiah. Mark, writing for a no-nonsense Roman audience, showed how Jesus got things done as the perfect servant of God. Luke, who appears to have written to a mixed audience of Jews and non-Jews, showed how Jesus was the perfect human being.

Matthew, Mark and Luke contain many of the same stories, and these stories are often presented in the same sequence. In some instances, the Gospel writers even maintain the same wording. Mark appears to have been the earliest Gospel written, as only 3 percent of the material is unique to that book while approximately 55 percent of its content can be found in Matthew and 42 percent in Luke. In addition, Luke and Matthew share some 25 percent of material not found in Mark, which has led scholars to believe that in addition to using Mark as a source, these Gospel writers had a secondary source (known only as the "Q" document, which is short for German *Quelle* or "source").

THE GOSPEL OF JOHN

Many scholars believe that John wrote his Gospel nearly a generation after the other three (somewhere between AD 80 and 100).[3] By this time, all or at least a majority of the other books in the New Testament had been written, and the life and work of Jesus were well known. The gospel of Christ had been preached in Jerusalem, Judea and Samaria and was spreading outward in every direction (see Acts 1:8). Paul, Peter and the other original disciples had suffered martyrdom, and the destruction of the Temple had led Jerusalem to be temporarily erased as a center of Jewish life. Additionally, false teachers were actively denying that Jesus Christ was the Son of God, come in the flesh.

According to the Early Church Fathers, the bishops of Asia requested John, in his old age, to write the Gospel in response to the teachings of Cerinthus, the Ebionites and other groups that were preaching heretical statements against Christ.[4] To this end, John's Gospel marches to a different beat, as he wrote to emphasize Jesus' divine power and glory. John's tone is more elevated and more exalted in view than the other Gospels. For instance, in Matthew and Luke, the titles "Son of David" and "Son of Man" link Christ to the earth, while in John, the title "Son of God" connects Him with the Father in heaven. John records no genealogy of Christ—neither His legal lineage through Joseph (as given by Matthew) nor His personal descent through Mary (as given by Luke). He gives no account of Jesus' birth or boyhood—his emphasis is how Christ was present "in the beginning."

Unlike the Synoptic Gospels, John tells us nothing about Christ's temptation in the wilderness (see Matthew 4:1-11; Mark 1:12-13; Luke 4:1-13). Jesus is presented as Christ the Lord, not the One who was tempted just as we are. In the Gospel of Luke, the author took care to guard our Lord's perfection in His humanity, but in the Gospel of John, the author guards Christ's deity. For this reason, he includes many accounts that reveal Christ's divine nature that are not found in the Synoptic Gospels, such as the Wedding at Cana (see John 2:1-12), the Samaritan Woman at the Well (4:1-42), and the Raising of Lazarus from the Dead (11:1-44). In John's day, as in ours, the deity of Christ Jesus had to be emphasized.

In John's Gospel, Jesus claims a special relationship with God. Thirty-five times He speaks of God as "my Father," while 25 times He asserts His divine authority through the statement "verily, verily" (*KJV*), a strong affirmation that indicated the importance of the teaching that was to follow. In John's Gospel, Jesus often personally affirms His own deity, and six other witnesses, both friends and enemies, also confirm His claims to deity.[5]

John's Great Prologue

John was one of the "sons of thunder" (Mark 3:17), and his great prologue—the first 18 verses of his Gospel—thunder throughout history with perhaps the most shocking, awe-inspiring and magnificent words ever written.

BEFORE TIME BEGAN

Some of the most important questions we can ever ask are, "Who was Jesus Christ? Was He only one of the world's greatest teachers? Was He merely one of the prophets? What did He actually do?" John launches into an answer of these questions by pointing to the existence of Jesus long before He ever started His public ministry and long before He was born in a stable in Bethlehem: "In the beginning was the Word, and the Word was with God, and the Word was God. He was with God in the beginning" (John 1:1-2). In this way, the Gospel opens much like the book of Genesis.

Here we must step lightly, for we are entering onto holy ground (see Exodus 3:5). The idea that Jesus was present from the beginning of the world is a profound mystery and one that unexpectedly and decisively shatters conventional wisdom. It is a truth that most likely slowly dawned on the disciples—and then only after they had ample time to digest the events surrounding Jesus' life, death and resurrection, the birth of the Church and the message of the Hebrew Bible in light of the events they had experienced. Yet even though this appears to have been a delayed realization, it is nonetheless an essential part of the gospel.

John chose his term for Christ, "the Word," very carefully. In the original Greek, this is the term *Logos,* which refers to a word that cuts sharply in two directions (see Hebrews 4:12, which also uses the term *Logos*). Christ came to declare God and tell about God. As words utter thoughts, so Christ utters God. As words reveal the heart, mind and personality, so Christ expresses and reveals God's heart, mind and personality.

The Jewish people in John's time had grown up confessing every day of their lives, "Hear, O Israel: The LORD our God, the LORD is one" (Deuteronomy 6:4). For them, "the Word of God" included God's commands, warnings and utterances to His people through the prophets. John's message in the opening verse of his Gospel would require a major rethinking on their part. John was saying that the *Logos* was "with" God and yet "was" God, indicating some sort of plurality yet unity within God. This teaching on the Word provided John with a base to explore and develop the understanding of the Trinity. John was stating that the eternal God has always existed as God the Father, God the Son, and God the Holy Spirit.

This same kind of radical mental adjustment would be asked of non-Jewish people who up until that time had regarded *Logos* as a lofty and abstract philosophical principle that integrated all reality. John infused the eternal *Logos* with personality. No longer would the governing principle of reality be impersonal; rather, the eternal "It" was revealed as tri-personal, again involving God the Father, God the Son, and God the Holy Spirit.

In this way, John invited his readers—regardless of their cultural background—to consider Jesus as more than the son of a carpenter, a prophet, an important messianic figure or the founder of a new way of thinking. Instead, he wanted them to connect the person of Jesus to the eternal person of God.

JESUS CHRIST AND CREATION

Just in case anybody missed the point about Jesus' eternal nature, John repeats the idea in verse 2: "He was with God in the beginning." Notice again that the *Logos* is not an "it"; John uses the personal pronoun "He." Next, John explicitly says, "Through him all things were made; without him nothing was made that has been made" (verse 3). God the Son, the Pre-Incarnate Christ, was with God during the creation of the universe.

In the book of Genesis, we find that the entire created order is not self-existent; rather, it comes from God, who created it out of nothing. As the author of Hebrews states, "By faith we understand that the universe was formed at God's command, so that what is seen was not made out of what was visible" (Hebrews 11:3). Throughout history, humans have worshiped the elements of creation, but John shows that God created the world and that only He is to be worshiped. Scientists try to understand where things came from, but in the end, they are faced with the miracle of God doing what only God can do.

In Paul's treatise in Colossians 1:16-17 on the supremacy of Christ, we read, "For in him all things were created: things in heaven and on earth, visible and invisible, whether thrones or powers or rulers or authorities; all things have been created through him and for him. He is before all things, and in him all things hold together." The universe was created by Christ and for Christ. Christ is the Word of God who holds the entire universe together. In these roles, Christ exhibits God's glory and is worthy to be worshiped!

LIFE AND LIGHT

In verse 4, John states, "In him was life, and that life was the light of all mankind." All life comes from God. Christ was with God in creation, and because everything was created by Christ and for Christ, all life comes from Him. Whether we believe in Christ or not, we owe our lives to Him.

But Christ isn't only the source of physical life. "Life" is a rich term that can speak of the quality of a person's life as a result of his or her faith (see John 5:40; 6:33-53; 6:63; 8:12; 10:10; 14:6; 20:31). John also speaks of "resurrection life," which is the promise of resurrection after death (see John 5:21-26; 11:25). "Eternal life" is another major theme in John's Gospel. Christ is the source of eternal life with God, and He came so "that everyone who believes may have eternal life in him" (John 3:15; see also 3:16,36; 4:14,36; 5:24,39; 6:27,40,47,54,68; 10:28; 12:25,50; 17:2-3).

Light and darkness also play a prominent role in John's Gospel. In the ancient world, light was seen as a symbol of purity and goodness, while darkness was seen as the evil in this world. Note that in using this imagery, John was not drawing on secular ideas in Greek philosophy but on the concept of light and darkness found in the Hebrew Bible. From the very beginning, the Bible identifies darkness as disorder and emptiness and light as good: "Now the earth was formless and empty, darkness was over the surface of the deep, and the Spirit of God was hovering over the waters. And God said, 'Let there be light,' and there was light. God saw that the light was good, and he separated the light from the darkness" (Gen. 1:1-4).

Spiritual darkness blinds people, but God turns "the darkness into light before them" (Isa. 42:16). John states that Christ is this Light who confounds, overcomes and dispels the spiritual darkness in our world (see John 1:4-9; 3:19-21; 5:35; 8:12; 9:4-5; 11:9-10; 12:35-36,46). When we follow Christ, our lives are filled with Christ's life and light. No matter how bad the darkness may seem, "The light shines in the darkness, and the darkness has not overcome it" (John 1:5).

JOHN THE BAPTIST AND THE LIGHT

John the Evangelist tells us that John the Baptist (a different John!) was not "the light"; rather, he was sent to point people to the Light, who was

Christ. Then John the Evangelist gets even more personal: "The true light that gives light to everyone was coming into the world. He was in the world, and though the world was made through him, the world did not recognize him" (1:9-10). God gives all of us some light, and we have the choice to move toward it or away from it. Notice that John says the general response of those in the world is to turn away.

How was Christ the Word received? Again, according to John, "He came to that which was his own, but his own did not receive him" (verse 11). Christ presented Himself as Messiah and King to the Jewish people, but a significant portion of the people rejected Him. In fact, all through the Gospel of John we see Jesus dividing the crowds. As He comes out and speaks the truth, the crowds listen to what He has to say. Some believe Him, while others reject Him. Tragedy indeed! But rejection is not foreordained, for some did come to the light. The door of faith is open to everyone (see Revelation 3:20).

JOHN'S GREAT PURPOSE

John does not hide the purpose of his Gospel but states it plainly in his opening: "To all who did receive him, to those who believed in his name, he gave the right to become children of God" (1:12). John stays on this message to the very end of his Gospel: "These [things] are written that you may believe that Jesus is the Messiah, the Son of God, and that by believing you may have life in his name" (20:31). For John, to receive Christ is to believe in Him, and to believe in Christ is to receive Him.

Note that the term "Jesus Christ" is not like our first and last names. Rather, "Christ" is a title, such as "His Honor." It comes from the Greek word *christos*, which is a translation of the Hebrew word *meshiach*, which means "Messiah" or "Anointed One." Jesus Christ is God's anointed King (see John 1:49). John's purpose in his Gospel is thus to convince everyone that Jesus is the Christ, the Messiah God promised to the Jewish people, the Savior of the world (see 4:42), and the unique Son of God. John wants to lead people who would believe into a life of divine friendship with Christ. He uses this key word, "believe," 98 times in his Gospel.

John states that those who accept Christ and become children of God are not born "of natural descent, nor of human decision or a husband's will, but born of God" (1:13). We do not have a natural right to be children of God—we must be *born* of Him (see 3:1-8). This new birth is a miracle that the God of creation can perform in our lives through faith.

JOHN'S GREAT THEME

John's great theme is that Jesus Christ is the divine Son of God, and he stresses this point more than any other writer in the Bible. In doing so, he reveals two astonishing truths in his Gospel: (1) the Word is God the Son, and (2) God the Son became a man.

Note that God did not send His Son into the world in order that He might *become* His Son, for Christ *has always been* the eternal Son. Our Lord had no beginning, for He is eternal and was present in the beginning. Christ was before all things, and because of this Jesus is not part of creation; rather, He is co-creator with God the Father and God the Spirit. Jesus makes visible the invisible God. As John reports, Jesus says that "God is Spirit" (4:24) and that "anyone who has seen me has seen the Father" (14:9). John himself says that Jesus discloses the unseen God (see 1:18).

Note that only in John's Gospel is Jesus called "the Word." Only here do we read about Christ's existence before creation and before He became a man. While the other Gospels focus on Christ's earthly life and ministry, John focuses on the cosmic Christ: "We beheld his glory, the glory as of the only begotten of the Father" (1:14, *KJV*). Jesus is "the Lamb of God who takes away the sin of the world" (1:29, *NASB*), the "Son of God" and the "king of Israel" (1:49), and the great "I AM" (8:58, referring to Exodus 3:14).

Christ's Mighty Deeds

Thus, in John's Gospel we see that Christ's mighty deeds began with creation and that they continue throughout human history as He sustains and upholds the universe. In addition, though we can't say with certainty, it is quite possible that between the time of creation and Jesus' ministry on earth He appeared to people in the Old Testament.

THEOPHANIES AND CHRISTOPHANIES

These appearances are often associated with the phrase "the angel of the LORD." Of course, just because a Bible story mentions angels or the "angel of the LORD" doesn't necessarily mean that it is speaking of Jesus Christ. The book of Hebrews tells us that angels are messengers for God, that the Son of God surpasses them, and that the angels actually worship Jesus Christ (see Hebrews 1). However, the Hebrew Bible describes several times when "the angel of the LORD" appeared and then, in the same story, states that "the LORD" spoke (see Genesis 16:7-13; 18:13-33; Exodus 3:2-14).

Students of the Bible call these appearances "theophanies" (God-manifestations) or "christophanies" (Christ-manifestations). The language around these incidents suggests that either (1) the angel of the Lord is speaking for the Lord, or (2) the Lord is speaking for Himself. And if the Lord is speaking for Himself—and God the Son is the Word of God—then it is not unreasonable to suppose that Christ Himself was present on at least some of these occasions.

CHRIST'S AUTHORITY AND SUBMISSION

Christ, as the Word, is the head over all creation, and He is also the promised Messianic King who brought redemption to the world and will bring all prophecy to fulfillment. In the book of Revelation, which many believe was penned by the same author as the Gospel of John, Christ is portrayed as the Lamb who has the authority to open the seals of prophecy and orchestate history to its final culmination (see Revelation 6).

As the Lord of nature and history, and as the Messiah and the Son of God, we would expect that miracles would accompany Jesus' life. But Christ's life was not all about receiving adulation and glory, for, as we shall see, it was also about submitting to His heavenly Father's will and walking the bitter path of humiliation to the cross. Although Jesus had all authority over creation, He submitted to the will of the Father and suffered on the cross to redeem humankind—His creation—and bring them back into relationship with Himself.

QUESTIONS FOR PERSONAL APPLICATION AND DISCUSSION

Each of the activities below is appropriate for personal study. These activities are also suitable as prompts for small-group discussion.

One of John's focuses in his Gospel is to show how Jesus the Son was present with God the Father at the time of creation. How did the Jewish people in John's time view "the Word of God"? Why would John's statement in his opening prologue have required a major rethinking on their part?

_____

_____

_____

_____

Philo of Alexandria (20 BC–AD 50), a Jewish philosopher, wrote that "the *Logos* of the living God is the bond of everything, holding all things together and binding all the parts, and prevents them from being dissolved and separated." How did John take this idea a step further? What is the *Logos*?

_____

_____

_____

_____

_____

In John 1:12-13, the Gospel writer tells us how we can obtain salvation from God. According to these verses, what has God done for us? What must we do in response? What will be the result if we follow what we read?

_____

_____

_____

_____

_____

According to John 1:13, what happens to a person when he or she makes the decision to receive Christ's salvation?

_____

_____

_____

_____

_____

The gospel has never been about merely stating the right things. In 1 Corinthians 2:14, Paul states, "When I came to you, I did not come with eloquence or human wisdom as I proclaimed to you the testimony about God. . . . My message and my preaching were not with wise and persuasive words, but with a demonstration of the Spirit's power." What is the relationship between works and words?

_____

_____

_____

_____

Some possible demonstrations of the Spirit's power include healings, cleansing from evil spirits, reconciliation to God and others through the cross, new social relationships between people, transformed lives and unusual circumstances that point to God's work overtly and behind the scenes. The Bible refers to these "attention getters" as "signs and wonders." These were present in Jesus' ministry and in the Early Church. How have you seen these present in your life today? What has "gotten your attention" about the gospel of Christ?

_____

_____

_____

_____

_____

The concept of light and darkness plays a prominent role in John's Gospel. Look up each of the passages below and write what John says about light and darkness. The first one has been done for you.

PASSAGE	WHAT THIS SAYS ABOUT LIGHT AND DARKNESS
John 1:4-9	Jesus is the light who came into the world to dispel the spiritual darkness, and the darkness will not overcome Him.
John 3:19-21	
John 8:12	
John 9:4-5	
John 11:9-10	
John 12:35-36	

In John's Gospel, "life" is a rich term that can refer to the quality of a person's life because of his or her faith, resurrection life, or eternal life. Look up the following passages and write down what they say about the life that Christ gives to us.

PASSAGE	WHAT THIS SAYS ABOUT LIFE
John 3:14-16	
John 4:14,36	
John 5:21-26	
John 6:33-40	
John 6:63	
John 10:10	
John 10:28	
John 11:25	
John 12:25,50	
John 17:2-3	

Only John refers to Jesus as "the Word," but he also refers to Christ in other ways. Look up the following passages and write what John says about Jesus.

PASSAGE	HOW CHRIST IS REPRESENTED
John 1:14	
John 1:29	
John 1:49	
John 8:58	

The Gospels are unique in world literature. They are not designed to bring the reader into acquaintance with facts about the important historical figure of Jesus Christ but are designed to bring the reader into a personal face-to-face encounter with the Lord Jesus Christ, who is every bit as much alive today as He was before He participated in the creation of the universe. Have you had this encounter yet in your life? If so, write a bit of your own gospel story here.

_____

_____

_____

_____

_____

_____

_____

_____

_____

_____

Notes

1. Eusebius, *Ecclesiastical History*, 3.39,14-17.
2. Other scholars date these later: Mark from AD 70–75 (immediately after the destruction of Jerusalem), Matthew from AD 80–90, and Luke from AD 90–100. Regardless of the dating, there is a general consensus among all biblical scholars that these four books represent the earliest and most accurate depiction of Jesus' life and ministry on earth.
3. Some scholars date John later, from AD 95–120.
4. Some modern-day scholars propose that the Gospel of John was written in stages by a community of believers who were personally close to the disciple John.
5. These witnesses were John the Baptist (see John 1:34); the disciple Nathanael (see John 1:49); Simon Peter (see John 6:68-69); Jewish opponents (see John 10:24-36); Martha (see John 11:24-27); and the disciple Thomas (see John 20:28).

Sources

Henrietta C. Mears, *What the Bible Is All About*, "Understanding John" (Ventura, CA: Regal Books, 2011), chapter 31.

Mears, *Highlights of Scripture Part Four: Words and Works of Jesus, Teacher's Book* (Los Angeles, CA: The Gospel Light Press, 1937).

GOD AMONG US

The Birth and Early Life of Christ (Matthew 1–4; Luke 1–4)

SESSION FOCUS

Jesus Christ became human and dwelt among us.

KEY VERSE TO MEMORIZE

The Word became flesh and made his dwelling among us.
We have seen his glory, the glory of the one and only Son, who came
from the Father, full of grace and truth.
JOHN 1:14

WEEKLY READING

DAY 1	Matthew 1–2
DAY 2	Luke 1–2
DAY 3	Matthew 3:1–4:11
DAY 4	Luke 3:1–4:13
DAY 5	Psalm 91

FOR LEADERS: SESSION AT A GLANCE

SESSION OUTLINE	60 MIN.	90 MIN.	WHAT YOU WILL DO
Getting started	10	15	Pray and worship
Main points of the chapter	25	35	Discuss the Incarnation and what Jesus did for us by becoming a human being
Application and discussion	15	25	Discuss personal application questions
Looking ahead	5	5	Prepare for next week
Wrapping up	5	10	Close with prayer or song

Jesus' Incarnation and Emptying

Now that we have examined Christ's presence from the beginning of time as presented in the Gospel of John, we will begin to look at His early life on earth, from His conception to His temptation in the wilderness, as presented in the Gospels of Matthew and Luke. One underlying theme in this account is the "Incarnation," which comes from two Latin words (*in* and *caro*) and means "to be made flesh." This is exactly what John was talking about in his Gospel when he says, "the Word became flesh" (John 1:14). God the Son, the Eternal Word, dwelt among us for some 33 years.

God became human in order to affect our redemption. In love, God the Son volunteered to redeem us from our sin and our rebellion against God. To do this, He was born into this world and went through childhood, His teenage years and on into young adulthood. He lived among people and ate, drank, laughed, sang and cried with them. He did signs and wonders, and His sublime teaching both rocked tradition and affirmed it. In this way, the Eternal Word became what He was not previously—a man. When this happened, He did not cease to be God: He was the God-Man.

A second underlying theme in the Gospel accounts of Jesus' early life emphasizes how He made Himself "nothing" for us. We see this in an early Christian hymn preserved in Paul's letters that urges believers to imitate Christ's example: "Who, being in very nature God, did not consider equality with God something to be used for his own advantage; rather, he made himself nothing by taking the nature of a servant, being made in human likeness. And being found in appearance as a man, he humbled himself by becoming obedient to death—even death on a cross!" (Philippians 2:6-8).

The phrase "made himself nothing" in this passage is translated from the Greek word *kenosis,* which means "the Emptying." The Eternal Word, in whom all the fullness of deity dwells (see Colossians 2:9), emptied Himself for us. He laid aside His divine privileges, took on human flesh, became God's Servant, and died for our sins. In His life He loved and served as an example for us to follow, and in His death on the cross, He poured out His lifeblood for us for our salvation. Jesus' Incarnation and Emptying are the pivotal point of all human history.

Jesus' Early Life

We learn about Christ's birth and boyhood in the Gospels of Luke and Matthew. We will begin with Luke, as his chronology starts a bit earlier.

A NOTE ON HISTORY

As we begin to examine the story of Christ's birth, it is important to note that the places mentioned in these accounts are not fictional—we know from historical sources and archaeological evidence that they actually existed. Jesus was born in Bethlehem of Judea, which was located in the "hill country" of Judah and is believed to be the same as the biblical Ephrath in the Old Testament (see Micah 5:2). He grew up in the region of Nazareth, located in the northern region of modern-day Israel. These are real places, and the towns still stand.

Similarly, the Gospels do not begin with "once upon a time." We set our Western calendars with abbreviations that stand for "before Christ" and *anno domini,* a Latin term meaning "in the year of our Lord." This dating system was devised in AD 525 by a Scythian monk name Dionysius Exiguus, who used it to compute the date of the Christian Easter festival rather than an actual historical event. In fact, current research performed after the fixing of Western calendars has shown that Jesus probably was born between 4 BC and 7 BC. Jesus was born in the days of King Herod "the Great," a client king of the Roman government known for his colossal building projects (including the Temple in Jerusalem) and his penchant for ruthlessness. History and archaeology attest to his deeds and his dreadful reign.

Luke is a careful historian. In his account of Jesus' birth, he goes well beyond the conventions of his time and gives six time markers for his story instead of just one or two: "In the fifteenth year of the reign of Tiberius Caesar—when Pontius Pilate was governor of Judea, Herod tetrarch of Galilee, his brother Philip tetrarch of Iturea and Traconitis, and Lysanias tetrarch of Abilene—during the high-priesthood of Annas and Caiaphas, the word of God came to John son of Zechariah [John the Baptist] in the wilderness" (3:1-2). Luke didn't just make up these people to give the story some credibility—they were actual officeholders at the time.

The Gospel narrative sets its record in the solid foundation of history. In this way, we can know that we are not building our faith on myth but on substantial fact. The events of the birth of Christ that Matthew and Luke depict were not done in a corner but in the broad daylight. The gospel is not afraid of the geographer's map or the historian's pen.

LUKE'S ACCOUNT: JESUS AS THE PERFECT MAN

As mentioned previously, Luke wrote his Gospel to an individual named Theophilus, a Greek name that means "God-lover" or "friend of God."

Luke was a physician, so he grounded his account in eyewitness testimony and personal research, stating, "I myself have carefully investigated everything from the beginning" (Luke 1:3). Throughout his Gospel, he brings a warm humanity into his task of presenting the Man Christ Jesus.

The tone of Luke's Gospel is different from John's. Whereas John begins with the Cosmic Christ ("In the beginning was the Word"), Luke begins with a simple, touching story: "In the time of Herod king of Judea, there was a priest named Zachariah" (verse 5). As the story unfolds, we are introduced to human sympathies and relationships of which none of the other Gospel writers inform us. We learn about the circumstances that accompanied Jesus' birth and childhood as well as the birth of his cousin, who, as it turns out, is His forerunner—John the Baptist (see 1:57-80).

Human interest pervades Luke's work. Only Luke tells us of the angels' song to the shepherds (see 2:8-20); Jesus' circumcision on the eighth day according to Jewish custom (see 2:21); Jesus' presentation, as firstborn son of Joseph and Mary, in the Temple (see 2:22-38); and the story of the boy Jesus, at 12 years of age, discussing Scripture with the elders in the Temple (see 2:41-52).

In Luke 2:1, the author notes that "in those days Caesar Augustus issued a decree that a census should be taken of the entire Roman world." Then he presents a fact that Matthew, with his emphasis on Jesus as King, would never mention: "[Joseph and Mary] went to their own town to register" (verse 3). In this way, Luke does not depict One who has claims to rule, but One who comes down in humility to this world to be involved fully in human affairs.

Luke connects the events of Jesus' life with what the Old Testament prophets had spoken about the coming Messiah. Micah had said that Bethlehem was to be the birthplace of a great and coming King whose origins were ancient: "Out of you will come for me one who will be ruler over Israel, whose origins are from of old, from ancient times" (Micah 5:2-5). However, Joseph and Mary lived in Nazareth, a town located 100 miles away from Bethlehem. Yet God saw to it that Imperial Rome sent forth a decree to compel Joseph and Mary to go to Bethlehem just as Jesus was to be born. Incredibly, God used the decree of a pagan monarch to bring His prophecies to fulfillment! God still moves the hand of rulers today to do His bidding.

In Luke, we hear the message of the angels to the watching shepherds, but we do not find the kings of the East asking for "the one who has been born king of the Jews" (Matthew 2:2). The angel tells the poor shepherds,

"I bring you good news that will cause great joy for all the people. Today in the town of David a Savior has been born to you; he is the Messiah, the Lord. This will be a sign to you: You will find a baby wrapped in cloths and lying in a manger" (Luke 2:10-12).

Luke writes that "The child grew . . . and the grace of God was on him" (Luke 2:40). When Jesus was 12 years old, He went up with His parents to the Festival of the Passover in Jerusalem, as every observant Jewish family was required to do. When the festival was over, Mary and Joseph returned home, but "the boy Jesus stayed behind in Jerusalem" (verse 43). How characteristic of a boy this is!

When Jesus' earthly parents discovered He was missing, they returned to Jerusalem where they found Him sitting in the midst of the rabbis, both listening and asking penetrating questions (see verse 46). Again, this is an intensely human depiction of our Lord. The rabbis and everyone who heard him were "amazed at his understanding and his answers" (verse 47). Then Luke records Jesus' first words: "Didn't you know I had to be in my Father's house?" (verse 49). This was Jesus' first self-witness to His deity.

After this, we read that Jesus went back to Nazareth with Mary and Joseph and was obedient to them. He grew in wisdom and stature, and found favor with God and men. All of these items pertain to Jesus as a man, and Luke alone records them. After this, 18 years of silence follow, and Mark and Luke record no further episodes from Jesus' life until He begins His public ministry. It is probable that Joseph died during this time, as nowhere is he mentioned again.[1] It is also possible that Jesus continued the family carpentry business until such time as his elder-son responsibilities to the family were completed (Matthew 13:55; Mark 6:3).[2] However, while the Bible doesn't give us much information about this time, we do know that Jesus took 30 years of preparation for 3 years of ministry.

MATTHEW'S ACCOUNT: JESUS AS KING

Jesus would have made it into any "who's who" book of notables. In Matthew's Gospel, the author provides a report on the greatest "Who" of history: Jesus the Messiah, God's anointed One, the Savior. Matthew's main purpose was to show how Jesus of Nazareth was the predicted Messiah and the Deliverer of whom Moses and the prophets wrote in the Old Testament. He was the One whom the prophet Isaiah, writing about 750 BC, predicted would be called, "Wonderful Counselor, Mighty God, Everlasting Father, Prince of Peace" (Isaiah 9:6).

The story of the birth of Jesus in Matthew differs from the record provided by Luke, although the two accounts complement one another. While there is much left untold, we do know that Jesus' earthly life began in a stable and that He had a manger for a cradle. His family and associates were humble folk, and He came into the world as a helpless babe. However, His birth was heralded by an archangel (see Matthew 1:20-21; Luke 1:26-38) and welcomed by an angel choir (see Luke 2:8-14). Furthermore, as Matthew tells us, He was worshiped by some of the earth's wisest philosophers (see Matthew 2:1-12). How divine was our Lord!

As we follow Matthew's account, we find that Christ had a *king's name* (see 1:23), a *king's position* (see 2:6), a *king's announcement* (see 3:3) and a *king's coronation* (see 3:17). Further emphasizing Christ's kingship, Matthew alone recounts the visit of the Magi (Greek *magos,* translated as "magician" or "wise men") from the East (Persia).

The Magi were most likely members of the priestly caste of Zoroastrianism, who, as part of their religion, were practicing astrologers who paid particular attention to the stars and were keenly interested in what might be portended in them. Along with much of the world at this time, they were expecting the advent of some great One. When they came to Bethlehem, they came to worship and honor this One: "Where is the one who has been born king of the Jews?" (2:2).

The question was on every lip. With all the prophecies that had been made to Israel, it is hard to fault the Jewish people (and the world) for expecting a King who would rule the earth from David's throne (see Jeremiah 23:3-6; 30:8-10; 33:14-16,25-26; Ezekiel 37:21; Isaiah 9:7; Hosea 3:4-5). However, the star led the wise men to a Person, not a creed. Their adoration foreshadowed Christ's universal dominion and the truth that one day "every knee [will] bow . . . and every tongue acknowledge that Jesus Christ is Lord, to the glory of God the Father" (Philippians 2:10-11). He is the one who would "rule from sea to sea and from the River to the ends of the earth" (Psalm 72:8).

Luke's and Matthew's Genealogies

Both Matthew's and Luke's Gospels contain something that is a bit foreign to us as modern readers: lengthy genealogical lists. While for us these genealogies might not represent the "exciting" portions of Jesus' early life, they do show how Jesus' birth fulfilled Old Testament prophecy concerning the coming Messiah. In this way, they serve an important function and have several important things to teach us.

In Matthew 1:1-17, we find the royal genealogy of the Son of David through Joseph; while in Luke 3:23-38, we are given Jesus' genealogy through Mary. In Matthew, Christ's genealogy is traced *forward* from Abraham, while in Luke it is followed *backward* to Adam. Notice in Luke 3:23 that it does not say that Jesus was the son of Joseph. Rather, Luke states that He "was the son, *so it was thought*, of Joseph" (emphasis added).

Why the differences in the two genealogies? The reason can be traced back to the purposes of the authors and their specific audiences. Matthew was concentrating on Jesus' relation to the Jewish people; thus, he had no need to go back any further than Abraham, the father of the Jewish people. Luke, writing to an audience that included Gentiles, was concentrating on Jesus' connection with the human race; thus, his genealogy had to go all the way back to Adam, the father of the human family.

In Matthew's genealogy, the royal line goes through David to Solomon, while in Luke it goes through David to Nathan. The Messiah had to be David's son and heir, as God had promised to David: "I will raise up your offspring to succeed you, your own flesh and blood, and I will establish his kingdom . . . I will establish the throne of his kingdom forever" (2 Samuel 7:12-13; see also Acts 2:30-31; Romans 1:3). The Messiah had to be a literal flesh-and-blood descendant, so Mary had to be a member of David's house as well as Joseph (see Luke 1:32).

Jesus' Baptism and Temptation

In Matthew's and Mark's Gospels, John the Baptist appears on the scene in an almost sensational way. The clothing he wore was made of camel hair, he wore a leather belt, and he had a strange diet that consisted of locusts and wild honey (see Matthew 1:4; Mark 1:6). There is a lesson here for us. If we were to select a herald for Christ, we would no doubt choose someone of high birth who was university trained and had a great reputation. Not so with God. John was of humble birth, was not an outstanding scholar, and dressed like a desert hermit. As Paul notes, God often picks "the foolish things of the world to shame the wise . . . the weak things of the world to shame the strong" (1 Corinthians 1:27).

John didn't go to people; rather, the people came to him. He didn't have any grandiose illusions about who he was, for God had told him that he would be the "voice" ushering in the coming of the Messiah that the prophet Isaiah had foretold hundreds of years before. As Isaiah had envisioned, the coming of the Messiah would be preceded by this voice who would cry out, "Prepare the way for the LORD; make straight in the desert a highway for our God" (Isaiah 40:3). This heralding voice would smooth the way for the coming King. It is amazing to find that it wasn't just Christ who was foretold in the Scriptures—God also included His forerunner, John the Baptist!

John preached repentance, and he performed a baptism of repentance. The act of repentance involves a person recognizing that he or she has done something wrong, admitting it to God and to the people he or she has harmed, confessing it, undoing the damage caused (as much as it is possible), and seeking forgiveness and reconciliation. Because sins involve other people, it can't just be something between a person and God.

John the Baptist understood that repentance and forgiveness go together, which is why his baptism was "a baptism of repentance for the forgiveness of sins" (Mark 1:4). John understood that if there were no repentance, it would be difficult for a person to get to forgiveness. Nor did he make it easy on people (see Matthew 3:7-10; Luke 3:7-9). He called the religious leaders of the day who came to see him a "brood of vipers." Much like the Old Testament prophets, he warned the people of the Day of the Lord and God's wrath against sin and His enemies. He said they shouldn't take for granted that they were okay with God just because they were "Abraham's children." God could raise up children from the stones if He wanted to do so—and there were lots of stones in the desert!

The people, concerned that they might be in big trouble, began to ask what they should do (see Luke 3:10-14). John told them to act ethically, treat each other with fairness and compassion, shun violence and be content with what they had. John showed them that their spiritual roads were full of chuckholes (washed out) and needed heavy-duty repair and rebuilding.

Matthew's, Mark's and Luke's Gospels tell us that John baptized Jesus (John 1:29-33 also points to the events of Jesus' baptism). Why? Jesus had never sinned, so He didn't need to repent, and He didn't need forgiveness. So what was He doing? In fact, baptism was Jesus' way of identifying with the people. He was showing them that even in their sin, He was with them. He was also prophetically demonstrating that He who had never sinned would become sin in order to reconcile people to God (see 2 Corinthians 5:21). In this way, Jesus is linked with "all the people," as He came down to the level of humans.

John the Baptist understood that Jesus was without sin, and he even tried to deter Jesus, saying, "I need to be baptized by you, and do you come to me?" (Matthew 3:13). He had previously stated that he was unworthy to unloose the straps of the Messiah's sandal (see Mark 1:7). John's baptism was only with water, but the One to come would baptize people with the Holy Spirit.

At the moment Jesus was baptized, the heavens opened, the Holy Spirit came upon Jesus, and a voice from heaven was heard saying, "You are My beloved Son, in You I am well-pleased" (Luke 3:22, *NASB*). In this, we see a picture of the Trinity: God the Father, God the Son, and God the Holy Spirit seamlessly working together. From a human standpoint, it had to be encouraging to Jesus to hear God say, "I am well-pleased with you, Son," and to be anointed in a powerful way with the Holy Spirit of God.

JESUS RESISTS THE DEVIL

Jesus' baptism marks the start of His public ministry, which Luke states began when He was "about thirty years old" (3:23). Hardly had the voice from heaven died away when we hear a whisper from hell. Out of the baptismal benediction of the Father, Jesus stepped into a desperate struggle with the devil. As Luke states, "Jesus, full of the Holy Spirit, left the Jordan and was led by the Spirit into the wilderness, where for forty days he was tempted by the devil" (Luke 4:1-2).

Satan's temptations were based, as they always are, on lies containing a grain of truth. Satan's first temptation directly challenged Jesus' fast; it had to do with getting Him to use His godly powers to meet His physical needs. After all, what would be the harm in performing a little miracle to accomplish this? Jesus countered by stating, "Man does not live on bread alone but on every word that comes from the mouth of the LORD" (Deuteronomy 8:3).

The second temptation had to do with Jesus (supposedly) trusting in God's protection. What would be wrong, Satan asked Him, if He were to fling Himself off the pinnacle of the Temple? Hadn't God promised to send angels to bear Him up, lest He even stub His toe (see Psalm 91:11-12)? Jesus recognized the temptation as presumption and answered, "Do not put the LORD your God to the test" (Deuteronomy 6:16).

Finally, Satan offered Jesus a shortcut to that universal Kingdom that God had promised to Him. Jesus could avoid the long and painful way of the cross! All He had to do was bow down and worship Satan, and everything would be okay. Jesus answered, "Worship the LORD your God, and him only shall you serve" (Deuteronomy 6:13, *ESV*). Jesus stood victorious, His shield undented and untarnished.

The purpose of Jesus enduring these temptations was not to discover whether or not He *would* yield to Satan, but to demonstrate that He *could not*. It proved that there was nothing in Christ to which Satan could appeal (see John 14:30). The more you crush a rose, the more its fragrance is recognized. The more the devil assaulted Christ, the more His perfections were revealed.

With this resounding victory, "Jesus returned to Galilee in the power of the Spirit" (Luke 4:14), showing that the old Serpent had utterly failed to break the fellowship of the Son of Man on earth with His Father in heaven. Now that Jesus had overcome these temptations, He would go forth to conquer all other temptations, until the time of His final victory and ascension to heaven as Lord of all.

PREPARATION THROUGH TESTING

Suffering and trials are as much a part of God's plan as are thrills and triumphs. Jesus was "led" into the wilderness to be tempted. This was no accident or evil fate but a divine appointment. Temptation has its place in this world, for we could never develop in our faith without it. There is nothing wrong in being tempted. The wrong begins when we begin to *consent* to it.

Note that we are not to run into temptation or seek it out of our own accord. Jesus did not go into the wilderness to be tempted of Himself, but was led there by the Spirit. You will find that the path of duty will take you through temptations, but, as Paul states, "No temptation has overtaken you except what is common to mankind. And God is faithful; he will not let you be tempted beyond what you can bear. But when you are tempted, he will also provide a way out so that you can endure it" (1 Corinthians 10:13). God always makes a way of escape!

QUESTIONS FOR PERSONAL APPLICATION AND DISCUSSION

In Old Testament times, a person's status in the community (and under the law) was linked to his family heritage. For this reason, a person had to be able to show that he or she belonged to a certain family and tribe. We see an example of this in Genesis 5:1, in which the family of Noah is traced back to Adam. Given this, why was it important for both Matthew and Luke to include a genealogy of Christ in their accounts?

_____

_____

_____

_____

_____

Read Matthew 1:1-17 and Luke 3:23-38. What similarities and differences do you notice in these genealogies? What is the reason for these differences in terms of what Matthew and Luke were seeking to emphasize in their Gospels?

_____

_____

_____

_____

_____

Whereas John begins his Gospel with an account of the Cosmic Christ, tracing His origins back to the beginning of time, Matthew and Luke begin with Jesus' early life on earth. In the following table, read each of the passages and then list how each of these accounts agrees in presenting certain truths about how and why Christ came into this world.

PASSAGE	TRUTH PRESENTED ABOUT CHRIST
Matthew 1:6; Luke 3:31	
Matthew 1:18-19; Luke 1:26-38	
Matthew 2:1; Luke 2:1-7	
Matthew 2:21-23; Luke 2:39	

In Luke 1:46-56, we find Mary's Song, which in Latin is called the *Magnificat*. Read the passage and allow yourself to feel Mary's faith. Based on her song, what motivated her actions and her willingness to be used by God?

_____

_____

_____

_____

_____

_____

The Magi who came to pay tribute to Jesus in Matthew's Gospel were most likely members of a priestly caste from Persia, a land to the east of Israel. Given Matthew's emphasis on presenting Christ as King, why did he include this story in his Gospel?

_____

_____

_____

_____

_____

_____

During Jesus' time, shepherds represented the lower classes of society. They lived in the countryside outside the cities, where they spent a somewhat solitary existence guarding their flocks. They were tough men used to hard work and the elements. Given Luke's emphasis on presenting Christ as the perfect man, why was it important for him to include the story of the angels announcing Christ's birth to the shepherds?

_____

_____

_____

_____

_____

_____

Each of the Gospels provides an account of John the Baptist (see Matthew 3:1-12; Mark 1:1-8; Luke 3:1-18; John 1:19-28). What is John's function in each of the Gospel accounts? What specific prophecy about the coming Messiah did he fulfill?

_____

_____

_____

_____

_____

_____

John's baptism was "a baptism of repentance for the forgiveness of sins" (Mark 1:4). However, we read that Jesus, who was without sin (and thus had no need to repent), went to John to be baptized. Why did He do this? In what way did John protest to being the one to baptize Jesus?

_____

_____

_____

_____

_____

_____

After Jesus' baptism, He went into the wilderness, where Satan tempted Him. In what three ways did Satan attempt to lure Christ from His mission on earth? What was the purpose of Jesus enduring these temptations?

_____

_____

_____

_____

_____

_____

The two great themes of this session are the Incarnation and the *Kenosis*. What do each of these terms mean? What comes to mind when you think of these words?

_____

_____

_____

_____

_____

Notes

1. There are several other reasons that support this conclusion. First, references made to Jesus' earthly family later in the Gospels name His mother, brothers and sisters, but not Joseph (see Matthew 12:47; 13:56; Mark 6:3). It is also interesting to note that Joseph is not mentioned in the Gospel of Mark or in any of the Pauline epistles. Second, when Jesus was on the cross, He committed His mother, Mary, to the care of His beloved disciple John (see John 19:26-27), which would have been His responsibility as the firstborn if His father had died. Third, under both Jewish and Roman law, it was the responsibility of family members to take away the body of an executed person, but the Gospels state that it was Joseph of Arimathea who did this (see Matthew 27:57-60; Mark 15:43; Luke 23:50-53; John 19:38-39). This last point has led some to believe that he might have been a relative of Jesus' family. Given this evidence, Joseph was probably older than Mary (some traditions state he was much older) and died before Jesus began His public ministry.

2. The Greek word translated as "carpenter" in Matthew 13:55 and Mark 6:3 is *tekton*, which is actually a more general word that could cover makers of objects in various materials (and even a builder). However, the fact that Jesus was a carpenter dates back to early Christian traditions, including accounts by Justin Martyr (c. AD 165), who wrote that Jesus made yokes and ploughs.

Sources

Henrietta C. Mears, *What the Bible Is All About*, "Understanding Matthew" and "Understanding John" (Ventura, CA: Regal Books, 2011), chapter 31.

Mears, *Highlights of Scripture Part Four: Words and Works of Jesus, Teacher's Book* (Los Angeles, CA: The Gospel Light Press, 1937).

WORKER OF WONDERS

Jesus' Miracles in His Early Ministry
(John 1–4; Mark 1–9)

SESSION FOCUS

Christ performed many miracles and acts of service while on earth.

KEY VERSE TO MEMORIZE

The Son of Man did not come to be served, but to serve, and to give his life as a ransom for many.
MARK 10:45

WEEKLY READING

DAY 1	John 1–2
DAY 2	John 3–4
DAY 3	Mark 1–3
DAY 4	Mark 4–6
DAY 5	Mark 7–9

FOR LEADERS: SESSION AT A GLANCE

SESSION OUTLINE	60 MIN.	90 MIN.	WHAT YOU WILL DO
Getting started	10	15	Pray and worship
Main points of the chapter	25	35	Discuss Jesus' mighty acts and their relevance to our lives
Application and discussion	15	25	Discuss personal application questions
Looking ahead	5	5	Prepare for next week
Wrapping up	5	10	Close with prayer or song

Jesus' Early Ministry in John's Gospel

In this session, we will trace the miracles that Jesus performed during the first part of His public ministry. Our chief guides in this will be John, the writer of the Gospel of John, and John Mark, the writer of the Gospel of Mark (see Acts 12:12,25). We will begin with John's Gospel, which gives us some unique insights into the early ministry of Jesus.

THE MIRACLE OF ANYTHING GOOD COMING FROM NAZARETH

In John 1:35-51, we find the story of how Jesus first began to gather His disciples. One of these men, Nathaniel, was the kind of fellow who spoke whatever was on his mind. When he found out that Jesus hailed from Nazareth—a town of which he had a low opinion—he said, "Nazareth! Can anything good come from there?" The others said to him, "Come and see" (verses 46-47). With this invitation, John challenges each of us who read his Gospel to find out for ourselves if the events he reports hold together.

Jesus revealed Nathaniel's heart to him, and when Nathaniel was surprised, He made a miraculous prediction. Referring to "Jacob's Ladder," the striking vision Jacob received of angels ascending and descending on a staircase to heaven (see Genesis 28:12), Jesus said that heaven would open and angels would ascend and descend on the Son of Man (Jesus' favorite name for Himself). In this amazing use of the Hebrew Bible, Jesus was saying that He was the gateway to heaven.

THE MIRACLE OF TURNING WATER INTO WINE

In John 2:1-11, Jesus attended a wedding at Cana, located up north in Galilee. His mother, Mary, was there, and so were His disciples. But there was a problem.

In those days weddings lasted several days, and it was the responsibility of the hosts to provide food and drink for the guests during their stay. To run out of wine during such an event meant lasting shame for the family holding the wedding. This was the exact situation the distraught hosts of this wedding in Cana were facing.[1]

Jesus' mother explained the situation to Jesus simply and with no overt request attached: "They have no more wine." To this Jesus responded, "My hour has not yet come," meaning He was waiting for the right "hour" (or time) to begin performing miracles. Mary, undaunted, told the attendants, "Do whatever He tells you" (verses 3-5). She was not demanding anything of Jesus, but her faith in His ability was certainly shining through.

So Jesus instructed the servants to fill the jars with water, which they did, and when they drew it out they found it had been transformed into wine. After Jesus performed this miracle, the master of the banquet drew the groom aside and said, "Everyone brings out the choice wine first and then the cheaper wine after the guests have had too much to drink; but you have saved the best till now" (verse 10).

What a beautiful picture of God's grace and timing! He brought the best wine to light up the life of the wedding party. The psalmist wrote, "[God gives] wine that gladdens human hearts" (Psalm 104:15), and Jesus provided that same service here. God gave a sweet affirmation of marriage in Genesis 2:24, and Jesus provided that same affirmation here. This miracle also draws attention to a metaphor that Jesus will soon make between the "old wine" of religious legalism and the "new wine" of life with Him (see Matthew 9:14-17; Mark 2:18-22; Luke 5:33-39).

In turning the water into wine, Jesus revealed His glory for the first time. The disciples would never forget it.

MIRACLES OF PROPHECY, HEALING AND KNOWLEDGE

A little later in John's Gospel, we find Jesus' actions down south, in Jerusalem, drawing a lot of attention (see John 2:13-25). Jesus had caused quite a commotion by chasing the moneychangers out of the Temple precincts with a whip, and when the religious authorities demanded that Jesus produce a sign (a miracle) that He had that kind of authority, Jesus cryptically told them, "Destroy this temple, and I will raise it again in three days" (verse 19).[2]

This answer caused the authorities to scoff at Him. "It has taken forty-six years to build this temple," they said, "and you are going to raise it in three days?" (verse 20). In fact, Jesus had been speaking in veiled language of His death and resurrection on the third day. At the Passover celebration, Jesus performed more "signs." Signs are miracles, often of healing, that are signposts pointing to Jesus as the Messiah.

John ends this passage with an astonishing statement that Jesus didn't entrust Himself to everyone because He knew what was in each person. We can't hide our hearts or secrets from Jesus. He can see right through us.

THE MIRACLE OF THE NEW BIRTH

In John 3:1-21, Jesus engaged in a dialogue with Nicodemus, an upstanding citizen at the time and a leader in the religious council, on the subject of the kingdom of God. Jesus told Nicodemus, "Very truly I tell you, no one can see the kingdom of God unless they are born again" (verse 3).

Intrigued, Nicodemus asked a clarification question: Did Jesus mean that a person had to go back into his or her mother's womb? So Jesus made it plain: He was talking about a spiritual rebirth, a change of heart that can only be accomplished by the Holy Spirit. To Jesus, being born again was just as much of a miracle as healings and deliverances from demonic powers.

After presenting this dialogue, John goes on to connect the miracle of the Incarnation and the miracle of the new birth through the miracle of faith, stating, "For God so loved the world that he gave his one and only Son, that whoever believes in him shall not perish but have eternal life." Have you been born again?

THE MIRACLE OF BREAKING DOWN SOCIAL BARRIERS

In Jesus' day, the Samaritans and the Jews didn't get along. The Jews considered the Samaritans to be half-breeds, and the Samaritans had a similar attitude toward the Jews.[3] Both sides considered the other unworthy of salvation. (The bad blood had a faint basis in history, but the main issue now was prejudice.)

Society in Jesus' time was also fairly segregated along gender lines. Men were not supposed to talk to women unless they were relatives, were introduced to them, or kept it on a business level (such as at a street market). Men were especially not to talk to women of bad reputation.

Thus, we see that when Jesus initiated a conversation with the Samaritan woman at the well in John 4, He was actually breaking three social barriers at once: (1) the racial (Jewish or Samaritan) barrier, (2) the gender (male or female) barrier, and (3) the reputation (good or bad) barrier. A long conversation ensued, during which Jesus revealed to this woman that He was the Messiah (see verses 25-26). When the disciples returned and questioned Jesus as to why He was talking with this woman, He told them to expand their visions: "Open your eyes and look at the fields [the people of every race, including the Samaritans]! They are ripe for harvest [are ready to respond to the gospel]" (verse 35).

To prove His point, Jesus accepted the invitation of the Samaritans to stay awhile, and He and His disciples stayed for two days. As Jesus predicted, many Samaritans came to believe in Him. For her part, the woman herself could not have made a clearer declaration of Jesus' universal mission to all peoples, saying, "This man really is the Savior of the world" (verse 42).

Jesus' Early Ministry in Mark's Gospel

At this point we will turn to Mark's record of Jesus' early ministry. In Mark 10:45, the author clearly sets forth his objective in writing his Gospel: "The Son of Man did not come to be served, but to serve, and to give his life as a ransom for many." Mark's aim was to plainly tell the facts about Jesus—especially His deeds.

MARK'S AUDIENCE

As stated previously, Mark wrote for Roman readers. The Romans valued common sense. Their religion had to be practical, and they had no interest in tracing beliefs back into the past. Legal genealogies and fulfillments of prophecy left them cold, and arguing the finer points of Scripture interpretation held no interest for them. They might have said, "I know nothing of your Scriptures, and care nothing for your peculiar notions, but I should be glad to hear a plain story of the life this man Jesus lived. Tell me what He did. Let me see Him just as He was." This is the mindset that Mark sought to reach through his Gospel.

MARK'S STEADFAST FOCUS

The skill of an artist lies in what he or she leaves out. An amateur often tries to crowd everything in, which can distract the audience from his or her main point. Mark's omissions in his Gospel are in harmony with his central purpose, and it is for this reason that he leaves out a number of the stories we find in the other Gospels.

For instance, Mark leaves out the birth narratives, because his purpose is in presenting Jesus as the perfect servant, and no one cares about the pedigree of a servant. His writing contains no visit of wise men, because a servant does not receive homage. There is no account of the boy Jesus in the Temple, because it is irrelevant to what the servant can accomplish today. There is also little preaching, because Mark wants to show Christ as a perfect workman.

Mark uses the Greek word *eutheos* 40 times in his Gospel. This can be translated as "immediately," "at once," "as soon as" and "without delay." This is a servant's word.

PREPARATION FOR SERVANTHOOD

Although the book of Mark skips over the first 30 years of Jesus' life, it does not mean that Jesus wasn't preparing for His ministry during this time. Preparation in life is needed, and Jesus' life certainly illustrated this fact. Just as the foundations of a lighthouse rest beneath the surface and the roots on a plant stretch down into the dark soil below, Jesus had spent those unseen years preparing for His time of service on earth. Moses had spent 40 years in the desert before he entered into his great work (see Acts 7:30). Amos spent his youth on a farm (see Amos 7:14-15). So too with Jesus! Thirty years in obscurity; three years of public ministry. Getting ready for our life's work is of tremendous importance. Don't chafe if it takes time.

WORKERS WITH JESUS

In Mark's Gospel, the Servant renders continuous and unbroken service. People were in darkness, and so He taught them. People were without hope, and so He cheered them. People were sick and suffering, and so He healed them. People were under the power of Satan, and so He freed them. People were sinful, so He pardoned and cleansed them.

In Mark 1, we read how Jesus called His disciples to follow Him and become "fishers of men" (1:17, *KJV*). It is interesting to note that Jesus never called any person from idleness—He called busy and industrious people to follow Him. These men received His call, and "at once they left their nets and followed him" (Mark 1:18). Too often, there is lost time between us hearing the call and responding to it. Our doing lags far behind our duty.

SERVANT AT WORK

After Jesus' baptism by John, His endorsement by the Father and His temptation by the devil, the Holy Spirit anointed Him with power. Then, as told in eight short chapters in Mark, He cast out demons (1:21-28), banished fevers (1:29-31), healed diverse diseases (1:32-34), made lepers whole (1:40-45), enabled paralytics to walk (2:1-12), cured a withered hand (3:1-5), healed multitudes (3:6-12), quelled a storm at sea (4:35-41), restored a maniac's mind (5:1-15), stopped a woman's hemorrhage of blood (5:21-34), brought a girl back to life (5:35-43), fed 5,000 people (6:32-44), walked on the sea (6:45-51), healed those who touched Him (6:53-56), opened the ears of the deaf and the mouths of those with speech pathologies (7:31-37), fed 4,000 people (8:1-9), and gave sight to the blind (8:22-26).

The action is rapid-fire and events appear to blend into each other before our very eyes. Mark's descriptions are abrupt, but He preserves many things for us that would otherwise have been lost. For instance, Mark tells us that Jesus gently took people "by the hand" (5:41; 8:23; 9:27) and little children "in his arms" (9:36). Mark tells us that Jesus was grieved or distressed (3:5). He sighed (7:24; 8:12), He loved (10:21), He was angry (3:5). As the author of Hebrews would later state, "We do not have a high priest who is unable to empathize with our weaknesses, but we have one who has been tempted in every way, just as we are—yet he did not sin" (Hebrews 4:15).

ONE SABBATH IN THE LIFE OF JESUS CHRIST

In Mark 1:21-34, we are given a glimpse of how Jesus spent one Sabbath. The Sabbath occurred on the seventh day of the week and was observed as a day of rest and worship. Among Jews of Jesus' time (and to this day), it went from sundown on Friday night to sundown on Saturday night. A day was reckoned from evening to evening, not morning to morning (as we normally think of days), or midnight to midnight (as our clocks count them).

Jesus and the disciples were in Capernaum, and after a night's rest they went to the synagogue, where Jesus began to teach. The people were amazed at His teaching because he taught them as one who "had authority," rather than citing previous rabbis, which is how the teachers of the law instructed. At one point, a man afflicted with a demon interrupted Jesus. Mark, in his typical rapid-fire style, relates how Jesus cast out the unclean spirit.

After the worship service, Jesus went with James and John to Peter's house, where He healed Peter's mother-in-law of a severe fever. The Sabbath afternoon was spent in quiet rest and friendly conversation. Toward evening time, as the twilight began to settle over the land, men and women approached the house, bringing with them great numbers of people sick with every kind of disease. The whole town gathered at their door, and Jesus laid His tender hands upon the sick and healed them. Imagine the scene: The lame jumped from their stretchers and leapt for joy; the blind opened their eyes to see their Healer; the lines in peoples' faces of long suffering turned into expressions of unbelievable happiness as one after another they were delivered from their painful diseases.

THE MEANING OF THE SABBATH

The fourth commandment that God gave to the people of Israel was to "remember the Sabbath day by keeping it holy" (Exodus 20:8), and in the

Hebrew Bible this law was strictly enforced. However, during Jesus' time on earth the religious establishment had added many extra laws regarding Sabbath-keeping, to the point where people could only take a certain number of steps on the Sabbath, along with many other rules. Absolutely no "work" was permitted.

Jesus had a relatively relaxed attitude by comparison toward the Sabbath. He allowed His disciples to rub stalks of grain together with their hands (to "thresh" grain, which was seen as "work"), and He healed (another type of "work") on the Sabbath. It might be hard for us to understand, but doing these things was actually controversial.

One time, Jesus went into the synagogue on the Sabbath and saw a man with a shriveled hand. He knew that the religious establishment was watching Him, so He told the man to stand up in front of everyone and then said, "Which is lawful on the Sabbath: to do good or to do evil, to save life or to kill?" (Mark 3:4). Jesus was saying that whatever we can do to help people—regardless of whether that happens to fall on the Sabbath—is in perfect harmony with God's design. Christ illustrated this truth with His own miracles, performing seven recorded healings on the Jewish day of rest.

Mark records a wonderful statement that Jesus made concerning the Sabbath: "The Sabbath was made for man, not man for the Sabbath" (2:27). This is the central principle of Sabbath observance. The Sabbath was God's gift to people. He did not create it to annoy, confine or impoverish people, but to enrich them and bless them! It is also interesting to note that after Christ rose from the dead "on the first day of the week" (John 20:1), which was a Sunday, Jewish believers in Jesus began the custom of worshiping on Sunday as well as the Sabbath. Today, in honor of the resurrection, the Christian "Sabbath" (the "Lord's Day") is held on Sunday.

THE SERVANT FORGIVES SIN

In Mark 2:1-12, we read that the news of Jesus' healing ability rapidly spread—without the benefit of press agents, newspapers, television, telephones, radios, the Internet or twitter. The friends of one paralytic man heard of this new prophet and decided to bring their friend to see Jesus. However, when they arrived, they could not get to Jesus because of the crowd. So they broke open the roof and lowered their friend down into His presence. Jesus said to the paralytic, "Son, your sins are forgiven."

When some of the teachers of the law heard this, they objected to the seeming blasphemy (direct offense against God) and said to themselves,

"Who can forgive sins but God alone?" In a sense, they were right. Sins are against God and, therefore, only God can forgive them. So Jesus gave them proof that He had God's own authority to forgive—to act not only as a physician of the body but also as a healer of the soul. Jesus knew in His spirit what they were thinking and said to those gathered, "I want you to know that the Son of Man has authority on earth to forgive sins." Then He said to the paralytic, "I tell you, get up, take your mat and go home."

Through this miracle, God validated Jesus' claim to be the Messiah. The man arose, took up his bed and went forth before them all. In this way, he served as a living witness to Jesus' power over sin and a visible illustration of the work He had come to do.

AUTHORITY OVER NATURE

As we noted earlier, Jesus not only performed miracles but also taught using many parables. One time after interpreting His parables, an exhausted Jesus got into a fishing boat to journey to the next city (and to escape the crowds!). On the way, the weary Teacher lay down in the stern of the boat and fell asleep on a cushion. As He slept, a violent storm arose on the Sea of Galilee. The disciples, certain they were about to perish, frantically woke Jesus and said, "Teacher, don't you care if we drown?" At a word from His lips the sea became calm, causing the disciples to say to each other, "Who is this? Even the wind and the waves obey him!" Jesus had power over the elements (see Mark 4:35-41).

AUTHORITY OVER UNCLEAN SPIRITS

Jesus travelled across the sea to the region of the Gerasenes, where He was met by a demon-possessed man. This man lived by himself among the tombs because no one could constrain him—he could break chains and leg irons apart—and night and day he would cry out and cut himself with stones. When the man saw Jesus, he ran up to him and said, "What do you want with me, Jesus, Son of the Most High God?" The demons (for there were many inside this man) recognized that Christ had authority over them and begged Him not to send them out of the area. So Jesus agreed to allow them to go into a herd of about 2,000 pigs on the hillside, which immediately rushed into the sea and were drowned.[4]

ANOTHER ROUND OF MIRACLES

After healing the demoniac, Jesus returned to Capernaum. There He healed a woman who had been sick for 12 years, and "while Jesus was still speaking" (5:35), some people arrived from the house of Jairus, the synagogue leader, and called upon Him to raise a child already lying in death.

From there, Jesus began a third preaching tour of Galilee. He sent forth the 12 disciples, two by two, on independent missions to do the same kinds of things that He had been doing (see Mark 6:7-13). After giving them some training, Jesus sent them out on an extensive missionary tour among the villages of Galilee (see Mark 6:12-13). On returning, they would gather around Jesus (probably at Capernaum, their regular rendezvous) and report everything to Him (see Mark 6:30). As is the case with us, they needed frequent talks with Christ to carry out their work. They needed His sympathy, approval, guidance and strength.

Jesus had gone aside into a desert to rest awhile (see Mark 6:31), but the crowds followed Him. Without a break, Jesus then fed 5,000 people who had gathered to hear Him teach (see Mark 6:32-44). Because it was late in the day and the area was remote, Jesus needed to feed the people, which He miraculously did from a boy's lunch of only five loaves and two fish. This is one of the most important miracles Jesus performed. In fact, it made such an impression on the Gospel writers that of Jesus' 35 recorded miracles, it is the only one that is included in all four Gospel accounts.

After the feeding of the 5,000, Mark records many more miracles of Christ and other interactions with the religious establishment of His day. At the conclusion of these miraculous events and teachings, we find a simple conversation between Jesus and Peter. Jesus asks Peter who people say He is, and Peter replies that some say He is John the Baptist, others say He is Elijah, and others think He is one of the other prophets. When Christ then asks Peter who *he* thinks He is, Peter states, "You are the Messiah" (Mark 8:29). Like the woman at the well in John 4, Peter had witnessed Christ's power and knew that He was who He claimed to be—the promised Messiah.

QUESTIONS FOR PERSONAL APPLICATION AND DISCUSSION

What was the purpose of Jesus performing the miracles, signs and wonders that are found in the Gospels?

_____

_____

_____

_____

In John's Gospel, we find that the first miracle Jesus performed was turning water into wine at the wedding of Cana. How did Jesus initially respond to Mary's request? In what way did Mary show her faith in Jesus?

_____

_____

_____

_____

Each of the Gospels records the story of Jesus overturning the tables of the moneychangers in the Temple. In John's account, however, the story is told at the beginning of the Gospel, which has caused many to believe that John is depicting a separate event from the other Gospel writers. Look up the following passages in Matthew, Mark and Luke and record the differences you find from the story in John 2:13-25.

MATTHEW 21:12-27	MARK 11:12-33	LUKE 19:45–20:8

What three barriers was Jesus breaking down when he initiated a conversation with the Samaritan woman in John 4? What was the result of Jesus' willingness to go against these cultural norms?

_____

_____

_____

_____

Read Mark 1:10-12. Who is helping Christ in this passage? With whom does Jesus say He will baptize us? What does this mean in our lives?

_____

_____

_____

_____

Our response to miracles is a test of our character. Read the following passages in Mark 5 and indicate the people's responses.

PASSAGE	PEOPLE'S RESPONSES
Mark 5:1-18	The shepherds in the region
	The healed man
	Those in the Decapolis
Mark 5:21-34	The disciples
	The healed woman
Mark 5:21-34	Jairus's household

Read Mark 1:35. Jesus had a custom of arising early in the morning and going outside of the city to a solitary place to pray. His work was growing rapidly, and He needed heavenly communion with His Father. Read each of the passages below and write down what it says about the importance of prayer.

PASSAGE	WHAT THIS SAYS ABOUT PRAYER
Matthew 7:7-8	
Luke 21:36	
Ephesians 6:18	
Philippians 4:6	
Colossians 4:2-4	
1 Thessalonians 5:16-18	
James 5:13-16	

Jesus also understood the importance of rest. Read Mark 6:30-31. What did Jesus say to the disciples in these verses? What relevance does that have to our lives today in terms of our Christian service?

_____

_____

_____

_____

_____

_____

Jesus came to give His life as "a ransom for many" (Mark 10:45). What is a "ransom," and when is it paid? Who gets ransomed from what? What did Jesus mean when He spoke of being a ransom for many?

_____

_____

_____

_____

_____

_____

Read Romans 3:23. According to this verse, who might need to be ransomed?

_____

_____

_____

_____

_____

_____

Jesus has more authority than we often think He does. Read Mark 4:35-41. How did Jesus demonstrate His authority in this passage? What was the disciples' response? What does this tell us about trusting Jesus with the storms in our lives?

_____

_____

_____

_____

_____

Were you surprised by any of the events in this session that were labeled "miracles"? Which ones? Why do those events truly represent miracles in Jesus' time and in our time today?

_____

_____

_____

_____

_____

_____

_____

Notes

1. Two other passages in the Bible that depict the events of such wedding celebrations include the story of Jacob marrying Leah and Rachel in Genesis 29:14-30 and the story of Samson's very brief marriage in Judges 14.

2. In Jesus' time, every Israelite who had reached the age of 20 was required to pay a Temple tax, and those who traveled long distances to get to Jerusalem could also purchase an animal for sacrifice at the Temple. Because foreign money (with foreign images) was not accepted at the Temple, the moneychangers provided the service of exchanging all currency for accepted "Temple coinage." The problem was that the moneychangers charged a high rate of exchange and assessed a charge for their services.

3. When Assyria conquered the Northern Kingdom of Israel in 722 BC, they deported a portion of the Israelite population and allowed other peoples from the empire to settle in the region. In this way, the people of Samaria became a mixed race, and they often incorporated pagan practices into their worship of the one true God. The Samaritans built a temple at Mount Gerizim during the fifth century BC, which was destroyed during the time of the Maccabeans in 110 BC. This is why the Samaritan woman states that her fathers "worship on this mountain" in John 4:20. (For more information, see session 9.)

4. Read the parallel accounts in Matthew 8:28-34 and Luke 8:26-39 and Jesus' other recorded cures of demoniacs in Matthew 9:32-33; 17:14-18; Mark 1:23-26 and Luke 9:38-42.

Sources

Henrietta C. Mears, *What the Bible Is All About*, "Understanding Mark" and "Understanding John" (Ventura, CA: Regal Books, 2011), chapters 29 and 31.

Mears, *Highlights of Scripture Part Four: Words and Works of Jesus, Teacher's Book* (Los Angeles, CA: The Gospel Light Press, 1937).

A GOD WHO CARES

Jesus' Works in His Later Ministry (Luke 9–19; John 9–11)

SESSION FOCUS

Jesus Christ is the perfect man.

KEY VERSE TO MEMORIZE

Then he said to the crowd, "If any of you wants to be my follower, you must turn from your selfish ways, take up your cross daily, and follow me."
LUKE 9:23, *NLT*

WEEKLY READING

DAY 1	Luke 9–11
DAY 2	Luke 12–14
DAY 3	Luke 15–17
DAY 4	Luke 18–19
DAY 5	John 9–11

FOR LEADERS: SESSION AT A GLANCE

SESSION OUTLINE	60 MIN.	90 MIN.	WHAT YOU WILL DO
Getting started	10	15	Pray and worship
Main points of the chapter	25	35	Discuss Jesus' later ministry and the implications for His followers today
Application and discussion	15	25	Discuss personal application questions
Looking ahead	5	5	Prepare for next week
Wrapping up	5	10	Close with prayer or song

Luke's Purpose and Focus

In this session, we will study the miracles that Jesus performed during the latter part of His public ministry. Our main pilot through this section will be Luke, the writer of both the Gospel of Luke and the book of Acts. Luke's books comprise a little more than one-quarter of the New Testament, which make him the greatest contributor to the New Testament (even more than Paul). We will also briefly examine passages in John's Gospel.

WHO WAS LUKE?

Paul referred to Luke as the "beloved physician" in Colossians 4:14 (*KJV*). He appears to have been one of Paul's missionary companions on his travels (see Acts 16:10-24; 2 Timothy 4:11). Luke was a keen observer of human nature and had a special concern for bringing out the human side of a story.

The Bible doesn't give us much information on Luke's background. The Church historian Eusebius, writing during the fourth century AD, said that Luke was from Antioch in Syria. Syrian Antioch was the capital of the Seleucid Empire, a center of Greek culture, and the location of the Antiochean church, which was the first missionary-sending church in history. Up until the time that church sent Paul and his missionary band to the non-Jewish world, the Christian movement had by and large been a Jewish message to a Jewish audience. However, with amazing cross-cultural foresight and vision, the church in Antioch commissioned Paul and his missionary band to introduce the gospel to the Gentile world (see Acts 13:1-3).

It is possible that Luke was not a Jew, as throughout his Gospel he takes the time to explain Jewish terms that may have been unfamiliar to non-Jewish audiences. In addition, when Paul lists his missionary companions in his letter to the Colossians, he states that "these are the only Jews among my co-workers for the kingdom of God." He doesn't mention Luke until a couple of verses later, which would indicate that he counted Luke among his Gentile co-workers (see Colossians 4:10-14). If Luke truly was non-Jewish, it would mean that he was the only Gentile author of any of the New Testament books.

Luke wrote his Gospel to communicate to a Greek audience. Just as God had been preparing the Jews and the Romans for the coming of Christ, God had also been preparing the Greeks. The Greeks differed from the Jews and Romans in many ways and possessed a wider cultural outlook. They loved beauty, rhetoric, theatre and philosophy. Luke, an educated Greek himself, was thus well fitted for his task.

LUKE'S UNIQUE PERSPECTIVE

People influenced by Greek philosophy spent at least some time thinking about what it meant to be a good person, and Luke was no exception to the rule. Luke writes his Gospel for sinners, highlighting Christ's perfection as a human being and His compassionate love in becoming a human to save them. He shows how God took on flesh in Christ and accommodated Himself to our frame. Because of this, as Luke demonstrates, He knows intimately what it means to be human.

Even so, Luke depicts Christ as being unique. There is a great difference between who Christ is as the Son of Man and who we are as the sons of men—between who Christ is as the Son of God and who we are as children of God. In Luke 1:35, the angel's statement to Mary that Jesus would be the "holy one to be born" refers to Christ's humanity. Our human nature is tainted by sin and is unclean from the start, and none of us is totally innocent (see Psalm 51:5). However, when the Son of God became incarnate, He was holy, perfect and pure.

OVERCOMING PRIDE AND PREJUDICE: A WORLD GOSPEL

In Israel's past, the Jewish people had known abject slavery under the Egyptians. After the events of the Exodus, they had undergone depredations from marauders from other nations. They had experienced a short-lived golden period with King David and King Solomon, but then, just as quickly, their fortunes had waned. After the nation divided into the northern kingdom of Israel and the southern kingdom of Judah, they came under the powers of Assyria, Babylonia, Medo-Persia, Greece and Rome.

While in exile and under foreign occupation, the Jewish people had sought to preserve their culture by setting themselves apart and being different. To this end, as we discussed in the previous section, they had added hundreds of additional laws to the original Mosaic Law. They regarded the Gentile nations as unjust, uncouth, unclean and as God's enemies, and they wanted nothing to do with them.

Against this backdrop, Luke shows Jesus as one who tore down the barriers between Jews and Gentiles and made repentance and faith the only conditions for admission into God's kingdom. In Luke 24:46-47, he records Jesus telling the people, "The Messiah will suffer and rise from the dead on the third day, and repentance and forgiveness of sins will be preached in his name to all nations, beginning at Jerusalem." Luke thus reveals that the gospel of Jesus Christ was not just one of the religions of the world. It was the living truth of God, which had been adapted to all nations and to all classes (see Romans 1:16). As the Son of Man, Christ looked after the needs of Gentiles just as much as He looked after the needs of the Jews.

Christ's Later Ministry

In the previous chapter, we saw how Jesus' ministry could be divided into an earlier and a later period. During the early part of His ministry, Jesus was more or less centered around the Sea of Galilee, making periodic forays southward to Jerusalem. During the later part of His ministry, however, Jesus was more oriented toward Judea, and especially Jerusalem.

JESUS' LATER MINISTRY AS RECORDED BY LUKE

Luke 9–19 depicts the events that occurred during the later part of Jesus' public ministry. In Luke 9:51-56, He begins by setting out for Jerusalem, where He rebukes the disciples for asking whether they should call down fire from heaven to destroy a Samaritan village. Jesus goes on to explain the cost of discipleship to them (see 9:57-62) and to commission 72 of His followers (70 in the *KJV*) to go ahead of Him to every town and place He was about to visit (see 10:1-24).

As Jesus neared the end of His ministry on earth, instructing His disciples became increasingly important. He taught them how to pray (see 11:1-13), warned them to be on guard against the teachings of the Pharisees (see 12:1-3), encouraged them to acknowledge Him before all people (see 12:4-11), and said that they did not need to worry for provision (see 12:22-34). He instructed on how to be watchful like servants waiting for their master (see 12:35-48), on how to interpret the times (see 12:54-59), and on faith (see 17:1-10). Throughout His ministry, He also took them aside and told them of His coming death (see Luke 9:22,43-48; 18:31-34), but the disciples did not understand what He was saying to them.

As Jesus traveled from place to place, He told simple stories to connect with His audience and illustrate the many profound truths that He wished to convey to them. Luke records many of these parables, including the parables of the Good Samaritan (see 10:25-37); the Rich Fool (see 12:13-21); the Fig Tree (see 13:1-9); the Great Banquet (see 14:15-24); the Lost Sheep, Lost Coin and Lost Son (see 15:1-32); the Shrewd Manager (see 16:1-14); the Rich Man and Lazarus (see 16:17-31); the Persistent Widow and the Unjust Judge (see 18:1-8); the Pharisee and the Tax Collector (see

18:9-14); and the parable of Delegated Authority (see 19:11-27). In Luke 13:18-30, Jesus told the Parable of the Mustard Seed and the Yeast, in which He focused on how to identify the kingdom of God (see also 17:20-37), and He also taught the people on matters such as hospitality (see 14:7-14) and the cost of being His disciple (see 14:25-35).

As in Mark's Gospel, Luke related many episodes in which Jesus confronted the religious establishment of His day. He refuted claims that He was drawing on demonic power to free people from demons (see 11:14-36), spoke out against many of the practices of the Pharisees (see 11:37-53), and went against their ideas of "work" on the Sabbath by performing healings (see 13:10-17; 14:1-6). Luke records other miracles of Jesus' healing, including the healing of the 10 men with leprosy (see 17:11-19) and the healing of a blind beggar (see 18:35-43).

Because Luke was concerned with depicting the humanness of Christ, he relates many stories of Jesus' personal interactions with His followers and others who sought Him out. We read of Jesus' stay at the home of Martha and Mary (see 10:38-42), His interactions with children (see 18:15-17), His conversation with a rich young ruler (see 18:18-30), and His exchange with a tax collector named Zacchaeus (see 19:1-10).

JESUS' LATER MINISTRY AS RECORDED BY JOHN

John records some additional events that took place during the later part of Jesus' public ministry in chapters 9–11 of his Gospel. These include a man born blind whom Jesus healed (see 9:1-12), the Pharisees' subsequent investigation of this healing (see 9:13-34), Jesus' teaching on spiritual blindness (see 9:35-41) and the Good Shepherd (see 10:1-21), and the raising of Lazarus (the brother of Martha and Mary) from the dead (see 11:1-44). Although not part of Jesus' ministry, in this section of John we also find rising opposition to Jesus' ministry, with some saying that Jesus is demon possessed (see 10:20), threats to stone Him to death for blasphemy against God (see 10:31-33), and plots to kill Him (11:45-57).

THE TRANSFER OF SPIRITUAL AUTHORITY

These lists above are not complete, but they do give us a bird's-eye view of the busy life of the Son of Man during His time on earth. Compassion was the key word in His ministry, and He trained His disciples to demonstrate that same kind of compassion in their interactions with people. We see this in Jesus' commissioning of His disciples.

In Luke's Gospel, we are told that when Jesus commissioned the twelve, "he sent them out to preach the kingdom of God and to heal the sick. . . . So they set out and went from village to village, proclaiming the good news and healing people everywhere" (Luke 9:2,6). In the next chapter, when Luke tells us of the commissioning of the 72 disciples, we read that they went out two by two, as before, and were given the same charge to heal the sick (see 10:9). When the disciples returned, they reported with joy that even the demons submitted to them in Jesus' name (see 10:17).

Notice that the disciples did the same kind of ministry that Jesus had been doing: preaching the kingdom of God, bringing peace, healing people of their diseases, and freeing people from unclean spirits. It was not just Jesus doing the healing and the works; His disciples were also involved. This transfer of spiritual authority was an impartation of God's power from Jesus to the disciples, which they received by faith. Both Jesus and the disciples had to trust in God the Father and God the Holy Spirit to do the miracles.

Jesus performed healings and other miracles by depending on the directions of the Father and through the power of the Holy Spirit, not by depending on His own initiative or His own divine nature. As the apostle Paul would later write, Jesus did not take advantage of His equality with God; rather, He laid aside His divine privileges to become a servant (see Philippians 2:6-7). In this way, He set up a pattern for all believers to follow. Just as Jesus needed to pay attention to the Father's initiative (see John 3:34; 5:19; 7:16; 8:28; 12:49-50; 14:10), so too must we. Just as Jesus needed to be filled with the Holy Spirit, so too must we (see John 14:16-20,26; 15:5; 16:13-14).

Jesus didn't just teach the disciples solid moral principles, but He gave them the opportunity to put those principles into practice and experience God's kingdom breaking into human history for themselves (see Luke 10:1-12,28,36-37; 11:35; 12:8-9; 14:25-33; 18:18-26). He was joyful and excited to hear the report of the 72 because He saw in those initial skirmishes the ultimate victory over the devil and all his works. "I saw Satan fall like lightning from heaven," He said to them. "I have given you authority to trample on snakes and scorpions and to overcome all the power of the enemy; nothing will harm you" (10:18-19).

The safest place we can be, in life or in death, is in the arms of the Savior!

THE CENTRALITY OF PRAYER

As the disciples witnessed Jesus' intimacy with the Father and the amazing acts of God that accompanied His ministry, they no doubt wanted to know the best way to model that intimacy and spiritual power in their own lives. In Luke 11:1-13, one of the disciples, perhaps motivated by this goal, asked Jesus to teach him how to pray. In response, Jesus gave him a pattern that has come to be known as "The Lord's Prayer." Jesus followed this with a teaching on how the disciples could ask God for things with "shameless audacity" because He was not some far-off being who was unwilling to be "awakened" by their requests. Jesus told the disciples to keep asking, seeking and knocking, because God wants to give good gifts to His children—especially the gift of the Holy Spirit.

KEEPING THE PEOPLE GUESSING

One time when Jesus healed a mute, people in the crowd immediately suspected that He was casting out demons by the power of Beelzebub (Satan). Others tested Him by asking for another "sign" from heaven (see Luke 11:14-28). Jesus answered the first charge by saying that the powers of darkness do not work to cast out each other and told them plainly that God's power had come upon them. Regarding signs, Jesus simply refused to produce more, telling them, "This is a wicked generation. It asks for a sign, but none will be given it except the sign of Jonah" (11:29).

Jesus refused to play the game by man-made rules, and people often didn't know what to make of Him. In instances such as this, He seemed to speak in riddles. What was "the sign of Jonah"? In fact, people wouldn't know until after the resurrection, and even after that event the reference would still require some interpretation. What Jesus was saying was that just as Jonah was spit out by the big fish after three days, so too Jesus would rise from the dead three days after His crucifixion.

Jesus also told the people that "something greater than Solomon is here" (11:31). What or who was He talking about in this case? And what did He mean by then saying that "something greater than Jonah is here" (11:32)? Jesus maintained control by being unpredictable and keeping people guessing.

HEAL, TEACH, HEAL, TEACH

As mentioned previously, Luke used two of Jesus' healings to show His priority on people and compassion over Sabbath rules. In the first instance, Jesus' healing of a crippled woman on the Sabbath served as a bridge into a rabbinical dispute, which then morphed into Jesus' teaching about the kingdom of God (see 13:10-17). In the second instance, Jesus' healing of a man with an abnormal swelling of the body served to bridge into a discussion on the appropriateness (on the Sabbath) of having as much compassion for a fellow human being as for an animal stranded in a ditch (see 14:1-6). Jesus put saving lives well above Sabbath rules.

OBJECT LESSONS ON FAITH

On His way to Jerusalem, Jesus was traveling along the border between Jewish and Samaritan territory when 10 men with leprosy met Him (see Luke 17:11-17). "Jesus, Master, have pity on us!" they cried out to Him. Jesus told them to show themselves to the priests, and as they went, they were healed. Only one of these men—a Samaritan—returned to give thanks. Jesus said, "Were not all ten cleansed? Where are the other nine? Has no one returned to give praise to God except this foreigner?" After this, Jesus said to the man, "Rise and go; your faith has made you well." Jesus was more than happy to heal foreigners, and when He did, He used their faith as an object lesson for His Jewish followers.

THE BLIND BEING HEALED

Each of the Gospels tells powerful stories of the blind being healed (see Matthew 20:29-34; Mark 10:46-52; Luke 18:35-43; John 9:1-41). These stories are not just wonderful stories of Jesus healing people's physical sight but also their spiritual sight. We all need our spiritual eyes to be healed so that we can see Jesus.

The story of Zacchaeus the tax collector in Luke 19:1-10 teaches us that before we even "see" Jesus, *He sees us*. Zacchaeus, a short man, had climbed into a tree so that he could better view Jesus and His entourage. When Jesus arrived at the tree He stopped short, looked up at Zacchaeus, and invited Himself to dinner. At dinner, a marvelous change of heart came over this tax collector. He pledged to refund anyone he had defrauded—plus penalties—and Jesus pronounced that salvation had come to that house. When Jesus' love gets ahold of a person, things cannot remain the same.

BIG CLAIMS, BIG PREDICTIONS

We have seen many big claims by Jesus, and in Luke 17:24 the Gospel writer gives us another: "For the Son of Man in his day will be like the lightning, which flashes and lights up the sky from one end to the other" (17:24). In using this language, Jesus was talking about the coming "day of the Son of Man" in exactly the same kind of dire terms that the Old Testament prophets spoke about the "day of the Lord" (see Isaiah 13:6,9; Ezekiel 30:3; Joel 1:15; 2:1,11; 3:14; Amos 5:18,20; Zephaniah 1:14; Zechariah 14:1; Malachi 4:5). This would be an unexpected judgment, just as in the days of Noah and Lot (see Luke 17:26-29).

It is sayings like these that force us to realize that Jesus wasn't just some great prophet who could foresee the future. In this passage, Jesus was clearly identifying His own day with the awful, dreadful, cataclysmic "day of the Lord." However, before these things would happen, Jesus made a prediction: "[The Son of Man] must suffer many things and be rejected by this generation" (17:25). This was not the first time Jesus had made this kind of prediction or anticipated the desire of some to murder Him. The following chart will give you some idea of how strongly this prediction plays in the Gospels.

EVENT	MATTHEW	MARK	LUKE	JOHN
First prediction of the cross	16:21-23	8:31-34	9:22	6:67-71
Second prediction of the cross	17:22-23	9:30-32	9:43-48	—
Third prediction of the cross	20:17-19	10:32-34	18:31-34	—
Parable of the wicked husbandmen	21:33-46	12:1-12	20:9-19	—
Statement of the sign of Jonah	12:38-41 (16:4)	—	11:29-32	
Claim that He would be crucified	26:1-2	—	—	—
Anointment for burial	26:6-13	14:6-9	—	—
Prediction that He would die in Jerusalem	—	—	13:32-33	—
Statement that He would suffer many things	—	8:31	17:25	—
Claim that He would rebuild this "temple" in three days	26:61 (27:63)	14:58 (15:29)	—	2:19-21
Prediction of His death during the Last Supper	26:26-29	14:22-25	—	—
Jesus' prayer in Gethsemane to be delivered from the cross	26:39	14:36	22:42	—
Other predictions/ anticipations	—	—	—	7:1; 12:25

These predictions show that Jesus was intensely aware of His mission during His time on earth and of what was awaiting Him at the cross. He went through suffering and death in obedience to the Father and because He loved us.

ANTICIPATING THE RESURRECTION

The predictions mentioned above are not just about the cross but are also about the hope of the resurrection. Jesus believed and taught in the resurrection of the dead, as did many believing Jews of His time. This promise that God would re-animate the bodies of the dead in "the resurrection" was present in the Hebrew Bible (see Daniel 12:1-3) and in other Jewish writings. One time when Jesus was at a dinner party, He affirmed the resurrection by enjoining His hosts to invite the crippled, the lame and the blind to their receptions so that they would be repaid "in the resurrection" (Luke 14:13-14; Mark 12:18-27). Jesus also defended the resurrection when He answered a tough question about who was married to whom in the resurrection (see Matthew 19:23-33).

Nowhere does the Old Testament explicitly say that the Messiah would rise from the dead on the third day. Given this, when Jesus said He would rise "on the third day," what was the source of this understanding? Perhaps Jesus was thinking of Hosea 6:2, which in Hebrew says, "After two days he will revive us; on the third day he will restore us, that we may live in his presence." The Aramaic translation is a little more explicit: "He will give us life in the days of consolations that will come; on the day of the resurrection of the dead he will raise us up." Jesus appears to have seen this verse as a sign pointing to His own resurrection—a resurrection that would begin to usher in the ultimate kingdom of God.

One of Jesus' greatest signs in anticipation of His own resurrection was the resurrection of Lazarus (see John 11). This story, told only in the Gospel of John, relates how Jesus' friend Lazarus became ill and died when Christ was away from Bethany. By the time Jesus arrived, Lazarus had been dead for four days. Jesus told Martha, Lazarus's sister, that her brother would rise again. When Martha answered that she knew he would rise again in the resurrection at the last day, Jesus explained that *He* was the resurrection and the life. After this, Jesus went to the tomb and commanded Lazarus to come out. Lazarus came forth, his hands and feet wrapped with strips of linen, and in this way a miracle for the ages was accomplished.

QUESTIONS FOR PERSONAL APPLICATION AND DISCUSSION

Read the first few verses of Luke's Gospel and of the book of Acts. What similarities do you find?

_____

_____

_____

_____

_____

As mentioned in this session, Luke is the Gospel for sinners. What do you think of when you hear that phrase? What is a "sinner"?

_____

_____

_____

_____

_____

According to the Bible, a sinner is not someone who is as bad as he or she can be, like the dregs of society, skid row bums, murderers or otherwise thoroughly depraved persons. Rather, sinners can be "respectable" folk who are successful in life and business and admired by their peers. In other words, the word "sinner" describes the human condition. In what ways do we see Luke's Gospel targeted at this group of people—which includes each of us?

_____

_____

_____

_____

_____

All the Gospels have a missionary intent—the purpose of each writer was to bring the reader into a personal relationship with Christ. As you are familiarizing yourself with the acts of Jesus Christ in this section of Luke and John, what insights are you receiving into Jesus Christ and who He is to you?

_____

_____

_____

_____

Look up each of the passages below that refer to the "day of the Lord." (Be sure to not just read those single verses, but also read around them to get the context of the passages.) Write down what each passage says about this coming event.

PASSAGE	HOW THIS DESCRIBES THE DAY OF THE LORD
Isaiah 13:6,9	
Ezekiel 30:3	
Joel 1:15	
Joel 2:1,11	
Amos 5:18,20	
Zephaniah 1:14	
Zechariah 14:1	
Malachi 4:5	

After reading each of these depictions in the Old Testament, what is your general impression of what the "day of the Lord" will be like? How does Jesus uses the phrase "the day of the Son of Man" in Luke 17:22-27?

_____
_____
_____
_____
_____

What was Jesus' purpose in commissioning the 12 disciples? What was His purpose in sending out the 72? Why do we see Jesus' training of His followers being accelerated in these later chapters in Luke and John?

_____
_____
_____
_____

When Jesus sent out His disciples, in each case He sent them to do the same kinds of things that He had been doing. They were to rely on the same heavenly Father and the same Holy Spirit on which Jesus Himself had been relying. What implications does this insight have for you in your understanding of Jesus as the Perfect Man?

_____

_____

_____

_____

_____

How about for your walk with God the Father, God the Son and God the Holy Spirit?

_____

_____

_____

_____

_____

Luke 9:23 in the *New American Standard Bible* reads, "And He was saying to them all, 'If anyone wishes to come after Me, he must deny himself, and take up his cross daily and follow Me.'" The *New Living Translation* reads, "Then he said to the crowd, 'If any of you wants to be my follower, you must turn from your selfish ways, take up your cross daily, and follow me.'" Given that Jesus knew the cross was ahead for Him, what do you think He was saying to us here?

_____

_____

_____

_____

_____

Sources

Henrietta C. Mears, *What the Bible Is All About*, "Understanding Luke" and "Understanding John" (Ventura, CA: Regal Books, 2011), chapters 30 and 31.

Mears, *Highlights of Scripture Part Four: Words and Works of Jesus*, Teacher's Book (Los Angeles, CA: The Gospel Light Press, 1937).

WHAT'S SO GOOD ABOUT GOOD FRIDAY?

*Jesus' Last Week on Earth (Matthew 21–27;
Mark 11–15; Luke 19–23; John 13–19)*

SESSION FOCUS
Jesus Christ is our reconciler.

KEY VERSE TO MEMORIZE

*We all, like sheep, have gone astray, each of us has turned to our own way;
and the LORD has laid on him the iniquity of us all.*
ISAIAH 53:6

WEEKLY READING

DAY 1	Matthew 21; 23; 24–25
DAY 2	Mark 14–15; John 13–14
DAY 3	Luke 22–23; John 16
DAY 4	Matthew 26–27; John 17
DAY 5	John 18–19

FOR LEADERS: SESSION AT A GLANCE

SESSION OUTLINE	60 MIN.	90 MIN.	WHAT YOU WILL DO
Getting started	10	15	Pray and worship
Main points of the chapter	25	35	Discuss Jesus' last week on earth and the implications for us
Application and discussion	15	25	Discuss personal application questions
Looking ahead	5	5	Prepare for next week
Wrapping up	5	10	Close with prayer or song

The Great Confession

In this session, we will study Jesus' deeds during His last week of life on earth. For this study, we will draw from all four Gospels. The Church refers to this week as Passion Week, which calls our attention to Christ's passionate love for God and for us.

LIFE'S MOST IMPORTANT QUESTION

On a quiet day far away from the busy crowds, Jesus asked His disciples this question: "Who do people say the Son of Man is?" The disciples responded by telling Jesus what they had heard others say: "Some say John the Baptist; others say Elijah; and still others, Jeremiah or one of the prophets." Jesus then turned the general question into a sharp personal inquiry: "What about you. . . . Who do you say I am?" (Matthew 16:13-15).

This question, first asked by an obscure Galilean in that far-off place, has come thundering down through the centuries. It is the most important question that can be asked of anyone, for what we think of Christ will determine who we are and what we do. More than anything else, our perception of Christ—and whether we consider Him the Messiah and Lord—will influence our lives and thoughts to our very core.

LIFE'S MOST IMPORTANT ANSWER

As we previously noted, the impulsive, fervent Peter answered Jesus' question by saying, "You are the Messiah, the Son of the living God." In forming this response, Peter grasped that Christ was the fulfillment of hundreds of scriptural prophecies. Peter's confession is called "the Great Confession" because it exalts Christ as the Son of God, lifts Him above ordinary humanity, and crowns Him with deity. Jesus' reply to Peter affirmed this fact: "Blessed are you, Simon son of Jonah, for this was not revealed to you by flesh and blood, but by my Father in heaven" (Matthew 16:16-17).

From this point on, Jesus begins to reveal new truths to this handful of disciples about His purpose—and theirs. Now the fateful shadow of the cross falls across the path of the disciples. Jesus begins to draw back the curtain on the future, telling them that His path must run straight into the hatred of "the elders, the chief priests and the teachers of the law" and then on to the terrible cross (16:21). But He also saw the glory of the resurrection morning and how He would be raised to life on the third day.

At this, Peter, who had just demonstrated understanding from above in his confession as to who Christ was, protests and says, "Never, Lord! . . .

This shall never happen to you!" Jesus replied, "Get behind me, Satan!" (16:22-23). Jesus understood that the cross was God's plan, but Peter had not yet comprehended this fact.

Jesus' Final Week on Earth

The last week of Jesus' life on earth was marked by the following sequence of events:

Day	Event	Gospel Account
Sunday	The Triumphal Entry into Jerusalem	Matthew 21:1-9; Mark 11:1-10; Luke 19:28-40
Monday	The Cleansing of the Temple	Mark 11:15-17; Luke 19:45-46; John 2:13-18
Tuesday	The Conflict Heats Up	Matthew 21:23-27
	The Mount of Olives Discourse	Matthew 24–25; Mark 13; Luke 21
Thursday	Last Evening Together	John 13–17
	The Last Supper	Matthew 26:26-29; Mark 14:22-25; Luke 22:15-20
	Arrest and Trials	Matthew 26; Mark 14; Luke 2
Friday	Scourging and Crucifixion	Matthew 27; Mark 15; Luke 23; John 18–19

THE TRIUMPHAL ENTRY INTO JERUSALEM

On the Sunday before Christ's crucifixion, there was a commotion in the town of Bethany and along the road leading to Jerusalem. Rumor had it that Jesus was going to enter the city of Jerusalem that day. People had begun gathering into crowds. Meanwhile, Jesus had sent His disciples to procure a donkey's colt. He soon mounted the colt, and the procession started.

This little parade could not be compared in magnificence to the great processions that have accompanied the coronation of a king or the inauguration of a president. However, it meant much more for the world, because in riding this colt into Jerusalem, Jesus for the first time was permitting Himself to be publicly recognized and acclaimed as the Son of David. The end was swiftly approaching, and Jesus knew that even if He were only to be rejected, He had to offer Himself as Israel's Messianic King.

In their initial enthusiasm, the people took off their cloaks and tore branches off palm and olive trees and spread them on the road before Him. Shouts of "Hosanna to the Son of David!" and "Blessed is he who comes in the name of the Lord!" reverberated through the city. It took courage for the people to say these things in Roman-occupied Jerusalem. It amounted to heresy against the state religion and treason against Caesar.

Jesus' entry was enigmatic. He was not entering the city as a triumphant conqueror—there was no sword in His hand or bloodstained banner floating over Him. His was a different mission!

That evening, the crowds dispersed and Jesus quietly returned to Bethany. Apparently, nothing had been accomplished in the way of making Jesus King. His kingdom had come relatively unnoticed, without publicists, pomp or pageantry. Christ had to come as the Savior, for only then could He come again as King of kings and Lord of lords.

THE CLEANSING OF THE TEMPLE

Jesus returned to Herod's Temple the next day. He made a whip out of cords and drove out the sheep, goats and merchants from the Temple. He overturned the moneychangers' tables and the seats of those who sold the animals, shouting that they had made God's house a den of thieves. This act did not endear Jesus to those who were making a nice profit on the religious goods trade around the Temple.

THE CONFLICT HEATS UP

A bitter controversy ensued. When Jesus continued to heal people in the Temple precincts, the chief priests and elders challenged His authority. "By what authority are you doing these things . . . and who gave you this authority?" they said. Jesus responded by asking a devastating question: "John's baptism—where did it come from? Was it from heaven, or of human origin?" (Matthew 21:23-24).

The leaders were afraid to answer the question in front of the people, because if they said "from heaven," they would be supporting John's role as the forerunner of Jesus as the Messiah; but if they said "of human origin," they would be going against the will of the people. So they wimped out and said, "We don't know." Consequently, Jesus refused to tell them from where His authority came.

At this point, the Pharisees (the religious faction of the people) and Sadducees (the "real world" faction allied with Herod and the Romans) tried to trap Jesus by using His own words against Him (see Matthew 22:15-33). First, the Pharisees asked Him if it was right to pay the imperial tax to Caesar. This was a tax to the emperor introduced in AD 6 that the Jews despised because it represented a sign of Roman dominance. If the religious leaders could provoke Jesus into speaking against the tax, they could level a charge of sedition against Him. However, if He said the tax was just, they could then discredit Him and claim that He was siding with Rome against the people.

Jesus, knowing their intent, asked them to bring a denarius to Him, which was the small silver coin used to pay the tax. "Whose image is this? And whose inscription?" He asked. On the one side the words "Tiberius Caesar Augustus, son of the divine Augustus" would have been inscribed, with the emperor's image, and on the other "Pontifex Maximus," a Latin term referring to the Roman imperial cult. Jesus said, "Give back to Caesar what is Caesar's, and to God what is God's." In giving this answer, Jesus recognized the authority of Rome to level taxes against its subjects, but recognized the greater authority of God over His people. They should give the Romans their tax money—but their allegiance and worship only to God.

The Sadducees took a turn next. This particular group did not believe in the resurrection, so their question was aimed at tripping Jesus up in this matter. Drawing on regulations given by God, they asked what would happen to a woman whose husband had died and had remarried her husband's brother, as required by the Law of Moses. What if there were seven brothers in the family, and each one had died in turn? To whom would she be married when the resurrection took place?

Jesus again sidestepped the trap by showing that their understanding of the Scriptures (and the power of God) was in error. "At the resurrection, people will neither marry nor be given in marriage," He said. Jesus then quoted from Exodus 3:6, showing that God is not the God of the dead but of the living. Abraham, Isaac and Jacob were alive in the sense of this eternal reality. The Sadducees' understanding and interpretation of Scripture were completely wrong.

The Pharisees asked two more questions to trap Christ, but Jesus again proved His superior knowledge of Scripture and evaded their snares (see Matthew 22:34-45). His responses thwarted their trickiness and made them lose face in the sight of the people, which so enraged them that they began plotting to kill Him (see Mark 11:18-19; 14:1; Luke 19:47-48). Then, in a series of "Woe to you, teachers of the law and Pharisees, you hypocrites!" passages, Jesus exposed these groups to public ridicule (see Matthew 23:1-36; Mark 12:37-40; Luke 21:45-47).

THE OLIVET DISCOURSE

On Tuesday evening, Jesus gave a teaching from the Mount of Olives on the things to come. He predicted the destruction of Herod's Jerusalem Temple, which was an extremely significant event in Jewish history and one that definitively proved that Jesus was a true prophet of God.

The fulfillment of this prophecy occurred in AD 70 when, in response to a Jewish revolt against Roman rule, the Roman general Titus besieged the city and conquered it. As Jesus said would happen, the Roman armies completely destroyed the Temple, and not one stone was left on another (except for the huge foundation stones in what is now known as the Wailing Wall). The Jews were banished from Jerusalem for centuries after this catastrophe, and as a result the center of Jewish civilization shifted from Jerusalem to Babylon and Baghdad.

In this teaching, known as "the Olivet Discourse," some of the events Jesus says will occur seem to point to the fall of Jerusalem, while others seem to refer to things that will occur at the end of history. These near-future and far-future events are "telescoped" together so that it is difficult to tell them apart.[1] A common theme in these endtime teachings is that we are to be ready for Jesus to return to earth a second time, this time as a King in glory (see Matthew 25; Mark 13:33-37; Luke 21:31-36). When Christ comes again in the last day, He will come as a judge (see John 12:44-50).

LAST EVENING TOGETHER

Last words are always important. In John 13–17, Jesus, anticipating the fact that He would be leaving His disciples, gave them some final instructions. This evening represents the "Holy of Holies" of Scripture.

During Jesus' time on earth, He had divided the Jewish people. Some had believed in Him, while others had rejected Him. Now, He was gathering His own around Him in an Upper Room. He wanted to comfort His disciples, for He knew how hard it would be for them after He was gone. They would be like sheep without a shepherd.

What a picture we are given in John 13:1-11! Jesus, the Son of God, girded with a towel and with a basin of water in His hands, began to wash His disciples' feet. This was a practice found in the hospitality customs of many cultures of the Middle East, especially in places where sandals were the chief footwear. However, the task was generally performed by a servant.[2] What great deed of Jesus could better illustrate what He was calling His followers to do? They were to serve in the same spirit as He had served them. Through His deeds, He was showing that greatness is always measured by service. There can be no loving others without living for others (see John 13:16-17).

After washing His disciples' feet, Jesus foretold His betrayal by Judas (see 13:18-30). When Judas went out into the night, it was night in his heart as well. Fellowship brings light, but sin brings darkness. Judas was a pitiable figure, for even though he had unsurpassed opportunities of knowing Jesus, he chose to reject the Lord. This is what unbelief can do. Belief means life, but unbelief means death.

After Jesus announced that He would be leaving, He gave His disciples a brand-new commandment: "Love one another. As I have loved you, so you must love one another. By this everyone will know that you are my disciples, if you love one another" (John 13:34-35). In this way, Jesus was showing that discipleship is tested not by the creeds we recite, the hymns we sing or the rituals we observe, but by our love for one another. The measure in which Christians love one another is the measure by which the world believes in them or their Christ.

CHRIST'S PROMISES TO HIS DISCIPLES
Jesus then told His disciples that He was going to His Father's house to prepare a place for them. "And if I go and prepare a place for you," He said, "I will come back and take you to be with me that you also may be where I am" (John 14:3). Jesus' cure for fear of death is that when we die, we are going home to the Father. How many hearts have been put to rest and how many eyes have been dried by these words!

Furthermore, even though Christ was to go away, He was not going to leave His disciples alone. God the Father and God the Son would send God the Holy Spirit, the Advocate, the Spirit of Truth, the Comforter (*KJV*), to abide with them (see John 14:26; 15:26). This is a most wonderful promise for any child of God!

Jesus continued to pile up the promises about the Holy Spirit in John 14–16. Unfortunately, few of us know the presence of the Holy Spirit in our lives. It is by the Holy Spirit's power that we live, can do anything that pleases God, or are able to believe for miracles great and small. God is tripersonal: Father, Son and Holy Spirit. Then, in John 14:27, Jesus revealed

His legacy to us: "Peace I leave with you, my peace I give unto you." The only peace we can enjoy in this world is His peace, and we receive this peace through the Holy Spirit.

In John 15, Jesus told His disciples the secret of the Christian life: "Remain in Me" ("Abide in me" in the *KJV*). Christ is the Vine and we are the branches—He is our source of life. As branches, we cannot sever ourselves from the Vine and hope to bear fruit. If we live and walk in Christ, we will bear fruit, but if we do not abide in Christ, the fruit will soon disappear.

In John 16, Jesus explained more about the role of the Holy Spirit. He told His disciples, "It is for your good that I am going away. Unless I go away, the Advocate [the Holy Spirit] will not come to you" (John 16:7). When the Holy Spirit came, He would convince people that they needed to get right with God, and He would glorify Jesus. This is the privilege and task that all Christians have been given through the power of the Holy Spirit: to allow God to speak through them and testify to the reality of Jesus Christ.

In John 17, Jesus prayed to the Father. As the disciples listened to His loving and solemn words, they would have heard Jesus' pledge to protect them (see John 17:11), sanctify them (17:17), make them one with Him (17:21), and let them share in His glory some day (17:24). If you want to truly understand the beauty and depth of these wonderful words, kneel and let the Son of God lead in prayer as you read aloud this seventeenth chapter of John.

THE LAST SUPPER

Jesus' last meal with His disciples was the Passover. The original Passover occurred the night before the Israelites escaped from Egypt, but this time Jesus infused the meal with new meaning. "This is my body given for you," He said to them, "the new covenant in my blood, which is poured out for you" (Luke 22:19-20). Jesus then instructed them to "do this in remembrance of me."

The earliest known mention of this observance after the time of Christ is found in 1 Corinthians 11:23-26, where Paul writes, "The Lord Jesus, on the night he was betrayed, took bread, and when he had given thanks, he broke it and said, 'This is my body, which is for you; do this in remembrance of me.' In the same way, after supper he took the cup, saying, 'This cup is the new covenant in my blood; do this, whenever you drink it, in remembrance of me.' For whenever you eat this bread and drink this cup, you proclaim the Lord's death until he comes." To this day, Christians continue to reenact the meal as a way of remembering what Jesus did for them on the cross. In various churches it is called Communion, the Lord's Supper, the Pascal Feast (or Pascha), the Eucharist (Greek for "thanksgiving") and the mass.

ARREST AND TRIALS

It is at this point in Gospel narratives that the authors begin to relate the sad series of events that ultimately led to Christ's death on the cross. We begin by finding the disciples arguing during the Last Supper over which one of them would be counted greatest in the kingdom of God (see Luke 22:24-27). Then Jesus tells Peter that before the next morning had dawned, He would deny three times that He ever knew Him (see 22:34).

Right after the Last Supper, Jesus brought His disciples with Him into the Garden of Gethsemane. The change from the scene in the Last Supper to Gethsemane is like going from warmth to cold and light to darkness. Only two hours had passed since Judas had left the supper table, and now he was ready to betray his best friend. Note that Judas was not forced to betray his Lord—he personally chose to betray Christ, and God used this treacherous act to fulfill prophecy. God did not cause Judas to sin, but Judas's betrayal was prophesied because it was going to happen. No one ever has to sin to carry out any of God's plans.

The hour had now come. Our Lord's earthly mission was at an end. Yet the greatest work remained: He had to die that He might glorify the Father and save the world from sin. He had come to give His life as a ransom for many, and now that purpose was about to be fulfilled. In all of these events leading to the cross, we see Jesus always poised, always gentle and always prepared for what was to come. He was not surprised when He heard the soldiers approach; in fact, He stepped forward to meet them. And the men fell back before His majesty (see John 18:6).

A notable miracle that doesn't happen is Jesus summoning 12 legions of angels to deliver Him from His fate, which Jesus states He could have done after Peter makes a rash decision to cut off one of the ears of the servant of the high priest (see Matthew 26:51-54; John 18:10-11). Jesus could have avoided the cross, but He didn't. He went through with it out of obedience to the Father and out of His love for us.

Three "trials" (more like "kangaroo courts") quickly followed. First, Jesus was taken to the hall of the high priest. Although He was bound as a captive, it is evident that He was the One in command of the situation throughout this terrible drama. He went forth as a voluntary sacrifice (see John 18:4) and deliberately tasted death for every person. Next, He was taken into the hall of Pontius Pilate, who was the prefect of the Roman province of Judea (see Luke 23:1-7). As a representative of the Roman government, he represented the true political power in the region.

When Pilate could find no basis to a charge against Christ, he sent Him to Herod Antipater, who ruled the Jewish territories as a client state of the Roman Empire (see Luke 23:8-11). Herod had begun his reign after the death of his father, Herod the Great, in 4 BC, and he was the one who had sentenced John the Baptist to beheading (see Matthew 14:6-11; Mark 6:19-28). Jesus faced charges of blasphemy against God (a religious offense against Jewish law) and treason against Caesar (a state offense against the Roman Empire). Both were capital crimes. Eventually, Jesus was delivered up to be crucified.

Except for John, all the disciples deserted Him. Even stalwart Peter, who previously had claimed that he would always stand beside Christ, ended up denying Him three times. At the moment of Peter's third denial, Jesus gave Peter a look of love that broke his heart (see Luke 22:54-62). It is a sad turn of events for these men who had been so close to Jesus during His years of ministry on earth. But before you start blaming them, look up and see where you are. Are you following Jesus closely? Are you denying Him through your actions? Can Christ count on you?

Scourging and Crucifixion

The sham trials are over and at last it is morning—and yet, it seems like night. It is the world's blackest hour. The soldiers scourge Jesus with whips, mock Jesus with a crown of thorns and a fake sceptre, and demand that He prophesy where the next blows will fall. Pilate, who now has charge of the execution after Herod sent Christ back to him, leads Jesus forth to the people and says, "Here is the man!" (John 19:5). The Creator of this universe, the Light and Life of the world, the holy One of God, was subjected to this type of abuse and mockery! Satan then incited the crowd to cry, "Crucify! Crucify!" (19:6-7).

Christ made His way along the Via Dolorosa (Latin for the "Way of Suffering") to the cross (see Luke 23:27-38). Luke tells us that the name of the hill on which Jesus died was Calvary, the Latin name for "Golgotha" (the "Place of the Skull"). The soldiers drove the nails into His hands and feet and placed an ironic placard on His cross that read, "This is Jesus,

King of the Jews" (Matthew 27:37). In this, we find a witness—be it only scorn—to Jesus' kingly claim. At the cross, we have hate's record at its worst and love's record at its best. People so hated Christ that they put Him to death, yet God so loved the world that He gave people life.

Three crosses spiked Calvary's hill. On one of them was a thief, who was being executed for his crimes. To this repentant, dying thief, Jesus makes an amazing promise: "Truly I tell you, today you will be with me in paradise" (Luke 23:43). Jesus couldn't make that promise and keep it unless He truly was God's Son.

After hanging on that cruel tree for six hours, the Savior died. His death was not the result of physical suffering alone but of a broken heart, for He bore the sins of the whole world. In John 19:30, we hear His triumphant cry: "It is finished!" He paid the penalty for our sin, thus becoming the world's Redeemer. The scene closes with the Son of Man crying with a loud voice, "Father, into your hands I commit my spirit" (Luke 23:46).

The World's Greatest Sin

Isaiah's great message was that the Son of God would become the Servant of God in order to die and redeem the world (see Isaiah 53). All four Gospels record how the sufferings of Jesus in Gethsemane and on Calvary fulfilled the prophecies of Isaiah. Christ was the suffering servant and died for us! He bore *our* sins in His own body on the tree (see 1 Peter 2:24).

Our faith is one of four letters instead of two. All the other religions say "do," but our Christian faith says "done." Our Savior has done all on the cross. He bore our sins, and when He gave up His life He said, "It is finished!" This was the shout of a conqueror. He had finished humankind's redemption. Nothing was left for people to do. Has this work been done in your heart?

The greatest sin of this age—and in every age—is to reject Jesus Christ. All who have heard the gospel must either accept the Lord as Savior or trample Him underfoot. The people of Jesus' day made their choice, and the people of our day must make theirs.

When we examine this Presence that shines forth in the Gospels—this vision of God in the flesh—we cannot just glance at it and then pass it by. Rather, it is like looking at a piece of art hanging in a museum—we need to study it to appreciate all that Christ has done for us. As we do, we need to consider who Jesus really is to us. Is it just a name we repeat, or does He truly represent the lord and master of our lives? Remember the question that Jesus asked Peter before the events that led to His crucifixion: "What about you. . . . Who do you say I am?" (Matthew 16:13-15). Ask that question of yourself today, for the truth is that no one can escape it. A neutral answer is impossible!

Questions for Personal Application and Discussion

Look again at the words of Isaiah 53:6, the key verse to memorize for this session. What emotions does this verse conjure up in your mind? What does the prophet mean when he states, "the LORD has laid on him the iniquity of us all"?

_____

_____

_____

_____

_____

How did the disciples respond when Jesus asked them who people said the Son of Man was? How did Peter respond when Christ asked who they thought He was? Why did Christ say this had been revealed to Him through the Father in heaven?

_____

_____

_____

_____

_____

_____

Why does this represent life's most important question?

_____

_____

_____

_____

_____

Review the story of the Triumphal Entry in Matthew 21:1-9. Now look up Zechariah 9:9 and Psalm 118:26. How did Jesus' entry into Jerusalem fulfill these prophecies? Why was this entry so unlike one we would expect from a king?

_____

_____

_____

_____

_____

What was the purpose of the Pharisees' question to Jesus about the imperial tax in Matthew 25:15-17? What were the Sadducees attempting to do in asking their question about the resurrection in Matthew 25:23-28? In what ways did Jesus' responses thwart their efforts?

_____

_____

_____

_____

In John 13, we read how Jesus girded Himself with a towel and washed His disciples' feet. What implications does this act have for Christian leaders or those who would aspire to Christian leadership?

_____

_____

_____

_____

Jesus speaks about the Holy Spirit a number of times in John 14–16. What did Jesus say that the Holy Spirit would do in the lives of His disciples? What does the Holy Spirit do in our lives today?

_____

_____

_____

_____

John records a number of other passages that relate to Jesus' teachings on the Holy Spirit. Look up the following verses and record what each states about God the Holy Spirit:

PASSAGE	WHAT THIS SAYS ABOUT THE HOLY SPIRIT
John 3:5-8	
John 3:34	
John 4:23-24	
John 6:63	
John 7:37-39	
John 14:7,26	
John 15:26	
John 16:7-15	
John 20:22	

Think about what Jesus did during Passion Week. Now, think about what Jesus could have done, but didn't. If Jesus had such authority and ability to work miracles, why was He so restrained during this crucial week?

_____

_____

_____

_____

_____

What ideas do these reflections give you regarding Jesus' mindset during that final week of His life on earth?

_____

_____

_____

_____

_____

In John 19:30, as Jesus was hanging on the cross, He cried out, "It is finished!" With this in mind, what does it mean that other religions say "do" but Christian faith says "done"?

_____

_____

_____

_____

_____

Based on what you learned in this session, what is "the world's greatest sin"? Do you agree or disagree with this statement?

_____

_____

_____

_____

_____

What is so good about Good Friday?

_____

_____

_____

_____

_____

Notes
   1. "Telescoping" refers to the way biblical prophecy was revealed to people. Oftentimes, what the prophets were describing represented "peaks" or significant events that would occur in the future without describing the "valleys" or lapses in time that would occur between those peaks. Thus, in the Olivet Discourse, Jesus could have been describing events that would occur both in the near future (the destruction of the Temple) and the far future (the time of the end).
   2. A good example of this practice can be found in 1 Samuel 25:41 (see also Genesis 18:4; 19:2; 24:32; 43:24).

Sources
Henrietta C. Mears, *What the Bible Is All About*, "Understanding Matthew," "Understanding Mark," "Understanding Luke," "Understanding John" (Ventura, CA: Regal Books, 2011), chapter 31.
Mears, *Highlights of Scripture Part Four: Words and Works of Jesus*, Teacher's Book (Los Angeles, CA: The Gospel Light Press, 1937).

THE SUPREMACY OF CHRIST

The Resurrection and Ascension (Matthew 28; Mark 16; Luke 24; John 20–21; Acts 1:1-11)

SESSION FOCUS
Jesus Christ is Lord over all creation.

KEY VERSE TO MEMORIZE

And he died for all, that those who live should no longer live for themselves but for him who died for them and was raised again.
2 CORINTHIANS 5:15

WEEKLY READING

DAY 1	Matthew 28
DAY 2	Mark 16
DAY 3	Luke 24
DAY 4	John 20–21
DAY 5	Acts 1

FOR LEADERS: SESSION AT A GLANCE

SESSION OUTLINE	60 MIN.	90 MIN.	WHAT YOU WILL DO
Getting started	10	15	Pray and worship
Main points of the chapter	25	35	Discuss the cross, Jesus' resurrection, and Jesus' ascension as to how they apply to our lives
Application and discussion	15	25	Discuss personal application questions
Looking ahead	5	5	Prepare for next week
Wrapping up	5	10	Close with prayer or song

The Purpose of the Cross

In the last session, we studied the bitterness of the cross. Jesus, the world's most perfect human being, was killed for us sinners. God's Son—the God-man, the Messianic King—experienced the humiliation of defeat and death on our behalf. His death seemed to usher in the triumph of evil and cynicism and the defeat of everything decent and good in the world.

And yet, as sixteenth-century Spanish composer Tomás Luis de Victoria once wrote, "*Sweet the wood, sweet the nails, bearing so sweet a burden.*" The cross has an almost unbearable sweetness about it. In the cross, God expressed His unmatchable love for the world. Through the cross, Christ expressed His everlasting love for those who would believe in Him. Through the cross, eternal reconciliation is made possible. The cross—the pivotal moment of human history—is a mystery bitter and sweet.

We find this same sentiment in hymns such as Robert Lowery's "Nothing but the Blood of Jesus," where he writes, "*Oh! Precious is the flow that makes me white as snow; No other fount I know, nothing but the blood of Jesus.*" To those who remain untouched by the meaning of the cross, these words sound strange and even macabre. But to those who have experienced the love of God through Christ's sacrifice, they are sacred treasures.

A CLUE TO THE MEANING OF THE UNIVERSE

The cross gives us a clue as to the meaning of the universe. Through it, we find that victory does not always go to the proud, that honor is not necessarily due to the powerful, and that the way God accomplishes His will in the world is not always obvious. Self-giving love is not to be despised, for God uses "the foolish things of the world to shame the wise" (1 Corinthians 1:27). He works through the poor and weak, not just through the well-placed and privileged shakers and movers. Sometimes, only through death can breakthroughs for love be made. This has proven true again and again throughout history—up to the present day—with thousands of Christians martyred every year simply for believing in Christ. We often don't hear about these deaths, because they occur to horribly oppressed people who do not have access to the megaphones of the media. Yet they happen every day nonetheless.

PROPHECIES FULFILLED

The mode of the Messiah's death had been foreshadowed by various types and symbols in the Hebrew Bible. For instance, the bronze serpent the Israelites lifted up in the wilderness to bring healing to the people signified that He would be lifted up to bring healing to all (see Numbers 21:4-9). The blood sprinkled on the altar in the Tabernacle (and later, the Temple) to atone for the people's sin pointed to a later perfect sacrifice whose blood would also be shed to atone for the sins of the world (Exodus 24:6; Hebrews 9:22).

Several of the psalms vividly captured the details of Jesus' crucifixion. In Psalm 69, David wrote that He was to suffer a broken heart, that He would look for pity but find none, and that He would be given only gall for food and vinegar for drink (see verses 19-21). In Psalm 22, David, writing from the perspective of the Messiah, states that He would be reproached and ridiculed (see verses 6-8); that He would be "poured out like water"; that His bones would be dislocated (see verse 14); that His hands and feet would be pierced (see verse 16); and that His tormentors would cast lots for His garments (see verse 18). God the Father would actually forsake God the Son, with whom He had been in fellowship for all eternity (see verse 1).

It is important to remember that Jesus *died*. His death was not faked, and He did not go into a "swoon" and then come out of it three days later. When the Roman soldiers, performing their grim crucifixion duty, went to break His bones so He would die more quickly, they found that He was already dead. To make sure, they pierced Jesus' side with a spear, and blood and water spilled out of His lifeless body (see John 19:32-35). A wealthy and upright man named Joseph of Arimathea, who himself was "waiting for the kingdom of God" (Luke 23:51), claimed Jesus' body and put it into his own family's tomb, fulfilling Isaiah's prophecy that He would be "assigned a grave with the wicked, and with the rich in his death" (Isaiah 53:9).

NOT THE END OF THE STORY

All of these incidents of the Messiah's death (and more) had been foretold in Jewish prophecy, but this did not represent the complete redemption story. Other passages of Hebrew Scripture—particularly the psalms—hinted strongly at Jesus' resurrection and the eventual honoring of this despised One by all nations.

In Psalm 16, David prophesied that God's Holy One (*NASB*; "faithful one" in the *NIV*) would not be abandoned to the grave or see decay (see 16:8-11). This verse was one of the key prophecies that Peter quoted during his first major sermon in Acts 2:23-32 and became a major theme in the Early Church's proclamation of the gospel (see Acts 13:34,37). Likewise, in Psalm 22 David speaks of the crucifixion, but then includes an extended passage at the end of the psalm that speaks of all nations honoring the one to whom all of this would take place: the Messiah. In addition, we have one of the most powerful Old Testament passages on the crucifixion, which also promised a resurrection, in Isaiah 52:13–53:12.

PROPHECY: ISAIAH 52:13-15	FULFILLMENT
See, my servant will act wisely; he will be raised and lifted up and highly exalted. Just as there were many who were appalled at him—his appearance was so disfigured beyond that of any human being and his form marred beyond human likeness—so he will sprinkle many nations, and kings will shut their mouths because of him. For what they were not told, they will see, and what they have not heard, they will understand.	Jesus acted wisely during His life. God raised Him up and highly exalted Him. But before that, He was so disfigured and marred on the cross that many were appalled (How could this happen to God's Anointed One?). Just as the Old Testament priests sprinkled the blood of animals on worshipers to cleanse them of their sin, so too the blood of God's servant will sprinkle nations. God's actions in salvation will silence kings and wise men.
PROPHECY: ISAIAH 53:1-12	FULFILLMENT
Who has believed our message and to whom has the arm of the LORD been revealed? He grew up before him like a tender shoot, and like a root out of dry ground. He had no beauty or majesty to attract us to him, nothing in his appearance that we should desire him. He was despised and rejected by mankind, a man of suffering, and familiar with pain. Like one from whom people hide their faces he was despised, and we held him in low esteem.	Not everyone will accept the message of the gospel. If we are to understand about Jesus, then God must reveal that knowledge to us. Jesus grew up before God like a tender shoot; He did not come from the high and mighty, nor did He inherit a place of privilege. He was not exceedingly handsome. He did not receive universal acclaim when He came but instead was despised and rejected. He was a "man of sorrows" (*KJV*) who was familiar with the pain of life.
Surely he took up our pain and bore our suffering, yet we considered him punished by God, stricken by him, and afflicted. But he was pierced for our transgressions, he was crushed for our iniquities; the punishment that brought us peace was on him, and by his wounds we are healed. We all, like sheep, have gone astray, each of us has turned to our own way; and	This servant of God took our pain and suffering upon Himself. We looked at Him (on the cross) and thought He had been cursed, because this was the punishment those who had been accursed received (see Deuteronomy 21:23). However, the truth is that it was for our sins that His body was pierced by nails and a spear; He died ("was crushed") for our wickedness. He took the punishment that we deserved, and by His wounds we

Prophecy: Isaiah 53:1-12 (cont'd)	Fulfillment
the LORD has laid on him the iniquity of us all.	can be healed. We are all sinners, each one of us. He took our sin upon Himself.
He was oppressed and afflicted, yet he did not open his mouth; he was led like a lamb to the slaughter, and as a sheep before its shearers is silent, so he did not open his mouth. By oppression and judgment he was taken away. Yet who of his generation protested? For he was cut off from the land of the living; for the transgression of my people he was punished. He was assigned a grave with the wicked, and with the rich in his death, though he had done no violence, nor was any deceit in his mouth.	John the Baptist recognized Jesus as "the Lamb of God who takes away the sins of the world" (John 1:29). Jesus did not defend Himself before His accusers, but was silent. His life was impeccable, His arrest was unjust, His trial was a travesty, and His crucifixion was a brutal miscarriage of justice. People actually called out for His blood ("Crucify him!" [Mark 15:13]). He died with two thieves on either side. His tomb was the tomb of Joseph of Arimathea, a rich man. He had done no one wrong, had never harmed anyone, and had never told a lie.
Yet it was the LORD's will to crush him and cause him to suffer, and though the LORD makes his life an offering for sin, he will see his offspring and prolong his days, and the will of the LORD will prosper in his hand. After he has suffered, he will see the light of life and be satisfied; by his knowledge my righteous servant will justify many, and he will bear their iniquities. Therefore I will give him a portion among the great, and he will divide the spoils with the strong, because he poured out his life unto death, and was numbered with the transgressors. For he bore the sin of many, and made intercession for the transgressors.	All of these things happened because it was God's will for Jesus to make His life a sacrifice for sin (complementing and fulfilling the Old Testament's sacrificial system). Therefore, God will reward Him: He will bring Him back to life and let Him see His "offspring" (believers). Jesus will be satisfied; He will make people acceptable and righteous before God. God will make Christ victorious because He "poured out his life unto death" (died for us) and was "numbered with the transgressors" (took our sin upon Himself). He bore our sins and prayed for sinners like us (in fact, the New Testament says He continues to pray for us).

To the Jewish people living before the time of Jesus, this passage would have seemed familiar but enigmatic. Given what we know happened to Jesus during His last week on earth, these prophecies are almost eerily accurate. Bear in mind that this was written by the inspiration of the Holy Spirit some 750 years before Christ.

The Empty Tomb

According to Mosaic Law, a person hanged on a tree was not allowed to remain there at night but was to be taken down and buried before sundown (see Deuteronomy 21:22-23). For this reason, Joseph of Arimathea requested permission from Pilate to take the body of Jesus for burial. Pilate granted this request, and Joseph had Jesus' body wrapped in a linen cloth and laid in a tomb. John records that Nicodemus, the man who had previously visited Jesus at night and inquired about being "born again" (see John 3:1-21), accompanied Joseph and brought a mixture of myrrh and aloes to include in the burial cloth, per Jewish custom (see John 19:39-40).

Jesus' body was laid in the tomb on Friday (Preparation Day), which was the day before the Sabbath. On the third day, Sunday, Mary Magdalene and other women came to anoint Jesus' body with spices.[1] According to Mark, the women were concerned as to who would move the heavy stone in front of the tomb, but when they arrived they found that it had already been rolled away (see Mark 16:2-4). The women entered the tomb, where they saw an angel who told them that Jesus had risen. The angel told them to go and tell the news to Jesus' disciples (see Matthew 28:5-7; Mark 16:5-7).[2]

So the women left and told these things to the 11 disciples and other followers of Christ. Luke states that the disciples did not believe their words because it "seemed to them like nonsense" (Luke 24:11). Peter, however, sprang up and ran straight to the tomb. John's Gospel states that the (perhaps younger) disciple John accompanied Peter and actually outran him to get there first (see John 20:3-4). When John arrived, he saw the strips of linen lying there by themselves, just as the women had said, but he did not venture inside. Peter, true to his nature, had no such hesitation and went immediately inside the tomb to see for himself (see Luke 24:9-12; John 20:3-8).

THE BEST NEWS EVER

It was true: Jesus *had* risen from the dead, just as the Old Testament (and Jesus Himself) had said He would. This was the supreme test of His Messiahship. People thought that He had died and that His kingdom had failed, but through the resurrection, God the Father showed that He had accepted Christ's sacrifice. When Christ rose again, He defeated our greatest enemies: sin, death and Satan. His resurrection also assured His disciples that He really was the promised Messiah.

The significance of the resurrection, like that of the cross, cannot be overestimated. Through the resurrection, Christ overcame death itself: "God raised him from the dead, freeing him from the agony of death, *because it was impossible for death to keep its hold on him*" (Acts 2:24, emphasis added). What is more, just as Christ united Himself to humanity through His life and death, so too we are united with Christ in His resurrection. Now we are able to live a new life (see Romans 6:4) and "bear fruit for God" (Romans 7:4). The fact that Christ rose from the dead grants Him the supremacy over all things (see Colossians 1:18-20). No religious leader in all history can compare to Christ.

THE POST-RESURRECTION APPEARANCES

Jesus' resurrection was different from the other resurrection stories told in the New Testament. The raising of Jarius's daughter (see Mark 5:35-43) and of Lazarus (John 11:43-44) were resuscitations from death to normal life, but when Jesus came forth from the tomb, something radically different occurred. Just as the butterfly leaves the chrysalis shell, Jesus' body had been changed from a natural, flesh-and-blood body to a glorified one. It was a body that could be touched (see Matthew 28:9; Luke 24:39; John 20:27) and one in which He could partake of meals with His disciples (see Mark 16:14-18; Luke 24:42; John 21:12-13). Yet He could also appear and disappear (see Luke 24:31,26; John 20:19,26), and at times His friends seemed to not be able to recognize Him (see Luke 24:16; John 20:14; 21:4).

The New Testament records 11 times that Jesus appeared to His disciples following His resurrection—to individuals, groups and larger crowds. His first two appearances were to Mary Magdalene and other women outside the tomb (see Matthew 28:8-10; Mark 16:9; John 20:11-18). Jesus also appeared to two disciples making their way to Emmaus (see Mark 16:12-13; Luke 24:13-35). In this encounter, Jesus showed these disciples that, as their resurrected Lord, He was just the same loving and understanding friend as He had been before His death. After Jesus' walk and conversation with them, these disciples urged Him to come in and spend the night with them. Jesus revealed who He was by lifting up the hands that had been pierced on the cross and broke the bread. Then they knew Him, but He vanished out of their sight.

Soon after, Jesus appeared to Simon Peter (see Luke 24:34) and then to 10 of the disciples in Jerusalem (Luke 24:36-43; Mark 16:14; John 20:19-23). Thomas was not with the other disciples at this time, and he did not believe that they had actually seen Christ. "Unless I see the nail marks in his hands," he said, "and put my finger where the nails were, and put my hand into his side, I will not believe" (John 20:25). A week later, Jesus appeared to Thomas along with the others. "Put your finger here; see my hands," He said. "Reach out your hand and put it into my side. Stop doubting and believe." All Thomas could say in response was "My Lord and my God!" (John 20:27-28).

Sometime after this, Jesus appeared to seven disciples by the Sea of Galilee who, apparently, were thinking of returning to fishing for a living (see John 21:1-14). He again appeared to the 11 disciples on a mountain in Galilee (see Matthew 28:16), and then, as Paul records, to 500 brethren at once (see 1 Corinthians 15:6). Then Jesus appeared to James, most likely the brother of Christ and early leader of the Church in Jerusalem (see 1 Corinthians 15:7); and finally to a little group on the Mount of Olives at the time of His ascension (see Luke 24:44-53).

It was during this last appearance, as Jesus put out His hand to bless them, that He was taken up into heaven (see Luke 24:50-53). Now He was no longer the *local* Christ, confined (like the rest of us) in time and space, but the *universal* Christ. Because of this, He could make the following promise to His disciples: "Surely I am with you always, to the very end of the age" (Matthew 28:20).

At the time of the ascension, Jesus had been on earth after His resurrection for a period of 40 days, appearing to His disciples and speaking with them about the kingdom of God (see Acts 1:3). The attitude of Jesus' friends and disciples was now so different from the despair and shame they had felt at the crucifixion. Now they could gather together in the Upper Room in Jerusalem and await the Father's promise of the Holy Spirit. As Jesus had said before He left them, "Do not leave Jerusalem, but wait for the gift my Father promised, which you have heard me speak about. For John baptized with water, but in a few days you will be baptized with the Holy Spirit" (Acts 1:4-5).

A NEW DAY FOR WORSHIP

Almost all the first believers in Jesus were Jewish. The Jewish day for worship was on the Sabbath, the seventh day of the week. By Jewish reckoning, that would be from sundown Friday to sundown on Saturday. Worship on the Sabbath was a big deal in the Bible. It was one of the Ten Commandments and was a day to be kept holy (see Exodus 20:8-11).

No work was to be done on the Sabbath on pain of death, and it was to be celebrated by all generations as a lasting covenant (see Exodus 31:13-16). Worship on the Sabbath was deeply embedded in the minds of Jewish people.

But something about the resurrection of Jesus shifted the believers' thinking. As previously stated, Jesus rose on Sunday, "the first day of the week" (Mark 16:2), and several of His post-resurrection appearances also occurred on Sunday. Because of this, the earliest Jewish believers, while keeping to the Jewish custom of worshiping on the Sabbath, also began to meet on Sundays to commemorate the resurrection. Sunday came to be known as "the Lord's day" (Revelation 1:10), the day on which communion was celebrated (see Acts 20:7), and the day on which collections for the poor were made (see 1 Corinthians 16:7). Eventually, worship on the Lord's Day displaced worship on the Sabbath—a surprising and significant move given the immense importance of the Sabbath in the Old Testament.

The Ascension

After the Servant had given His life as a ransom for many, He rose from the dead. But Jesus didn't *just* rise from the dead, as stupendous an act as that is. As the Apostle's Creed states, "On the third day He rose again. He ascended into heaven and is seated at the right hand of the Father. He will come again to judge the living and the dead."[3]

The Ascension is rarely preached and often forgotten, but it is a benchmark of the Early Church's gospel, and so we should value it as well. Jesus was received into heaven to sit at the right hand of God the Father (see Mark 16:19), the place of greatest power and authority. He who had taken upon Himself the form of a servant was now highly exalted (see Philippians 2:7-9). The implications are far reaching.

THE GREAT COMMISSION

Before Jesus ascended to heaven, He gave the disciples what has become known as the Great Commission (see Matthew 28:18-20; Mark 16:15). Jesus said, "All authority in heaven and on earth has been given to me," and based on that authority, Jesus was now commanding His disciples to "go and make disciples of all nations." Here we have encapsulated the Church's missionary mandate: The gospel is not to be kept secret but to be taken to all ethnic groups throughout the world. Christ promises to be with us in this task "to the very end of the age." Risen from the dead and seated with the Father, He is yet the Wonder-worker (see Mark 16:20). The command rings with urgency. Not a corner of the world is to be left unvisited—not a soul is to be left out!

CHRIST'S INTERCESSION

In Romans 8:31-37, the apostle Paul states that we are more than conquerors through Christ and that He is actually praying for us. He is not only our defense attorney (see 1 John 2:1), but He also is actually praying for our success! As the writer of Hebrews states, "Therefore he is able to save completely those who come to God through him, because he always lives to intercede for them" (Hebrews 7:25).

CHRIST WITHIN US

The promise for believers is that just as Jesus promised to work with the disciples (see Mark 16:20), He is also working in us and through us. We are redeemed to serve God and others, and we are laborers together with Christ (see 1 Corinthians 3:9). "Therefore, my dear brothers, stand firm. Let nothing move you. Always give yourselves fully to the work of the Lord, because you know that your labor in the Lord is not in vain" (1 Corinthians 15:58).

THE GIFT OF THE HOLY SPIRIT

The gift of the Holy Spirit is made possible because Jesus ascended to the Father. As He said to His disciples, "Very truly I tell you, it is for your good that I am going away. Unless I go away, the Advocate [Holy Spirit] will not come to you; but if I go, I will send him to you" (John 16:7).

JESUS IS LORD!

The testimony of the Early Church—and our testimony as well—is not just that Jesus is Savior but also that He is Lord over death, Lord of heaven and earth, and Lord of human history. In the final analysis, after all is said and done, He will get the glory. "Therefore God exalted him to the highest place and gave him the name that is above every name, that at the name of Jesus every knee should bow, in heaven and on earth and under the earth, and every tongue acknowledge that Jesus Christ is Lord, to the glory of God the Father" (Philippians 2:9-11).

QUESTIONS FOR PERSONAL APPLICATION AND DISCUSSION

In what way is the cross both "bitter" and "sweet"? How does the cross provide a clue to the meaning of the universe?

_____

_____

_____

_____

_____

Read each of the prophecies listed in Psalm 22 and the passages listed in the New Testament. In the right-hand column, write down how each prophecy was fulfilled based on the New Testament passage you read.

PROPHECY	NEW TESTAMENT	HOW THE PROPHECY WAS FULFILLED
Psalm 22:6-7	Mark 15:16-20; Luke 23:35-36	
Psalm 22:8	Matthew 27:43; Luke 23:37	
Psalm 22:14	John 19:32-34	
Psalm 22:15	John 19:28	
Psalm 22:16	John 20:24-27	
Psalm 22:17-18	Matthew 27:35-36; John 19:24	
Psalm 22:1	Matthew 27:46; Mark 15:34	
Psalm 22:27-28	Philippians 2:10-11	

At the time of Jesus, Jewish law and custom severely limited the status and freedoms of women in Israel. Most women had little or no authority, and they were not allowed to testify in court trials. Despite this, in John 20:11-18 we read that the first person to whom Jesus appeared after His resurrection was a woman—Mary Magdalene. Why is this surprising? How does it reflect the overall way that Jesus treated women during His ministry (see Luke 8:1-3; 20:45-47; John 4)?

_____

_____

_____

_____

_____

_____

Read Paul's synopsis of the resurrection in 1 Corinthians 15:1-11. What are the main points that Paul cites as being of "first importance" in verses 3-5? How many resurrection appearances does Paul include? Why did Paul include this detail in his letter?

_____

_____

_____

_____

_____

Now read 1 Corinthians 15:12-19. What does Paul state about the importance of Christ's resurrection in this passage? What is the relation between Christ's resurrection and our ultimate resurrection (eternal life in Him)?

_____

_____

_____

_____

_____

Read the story of Thomas in John 20:19-29. Notice that Jesus doesn't condemn Thomas for being late to the previous meeting or for doubting. What does this story tell you about the place of doubt in faith?

_____

_____

_____

_____

_____

In John 21:1-14, Jesus gives Peter, the disciple who denied Him three times, the opportunity to confess Him three times. Jesus restored Peter to the full privileges of service again. What was the essence of Peter's confession?

_____

_____

_____

_____

The cross, resurrection and ascension of Christ are the bedrock foundation of Christian faith. Read Ephesians 2:4-7. According to this passage, what has God done for us? Where are we now seated, spiritually speaking?

_____

_____

_____

_____

_____

Read Romans 8:26 and Hebrews 7:23-27. Each of these passages refers to the Holy Spirit *and* Christ "interceding" for us. The word "intercede" means to interpose oneself between, which could mean between us and the Father (as in Him being our Advocate) or between us and the challenges and obstacles in our lives. How does the resurrection of Christ play a part in this (see Hebrews 7:24)? What hope can you derive from knowing that Christ Himself is praying for you?

_____

_____

_____

_____

_____

Read Colossians 1:18-20. Why does the resurrection grant Christ supremacy over all the cosmos? In what ways was the resurrection the "supreme test" of Jesus' Messiahship? What did Jesus defeat through His resurrection?

_____

_____

_____

_____

_____

In what ways have you made Christ supreme in every area of your life? (This might be a good time to write out a prayer!)

_____

_____

_____

_____

_____

_____

As you conclude this portion of the study, what are some new insights you have learned about the works that Jesus did while on earth?

_____

_____

_____

_____

_____

_____

Notes

1. All four Gospels state that Mary Magdalene, a woman from whom Christ had cast out seven demons (see Mark 16:9; Luke 8:2), was among the first to find that He had risen from the dead. Matthew states that she was accompanied by "the other Mary" (Matthew 28:1); Mark lists her companions as "Mary the mother of James, and Salome" (Mark 16:1); Luke lists "Joanna, Mary the mother of James and the others" (Luke 24:10). John lists only Mary Magdalene (see John 20:1).
2. Luke records that the women saw two angels, who reminded them what Jesus had previously said to them: "The Son of Man must be delivered over to the hands of sinners, be crucified and on the third day be raised again" (see Luke 24:4-7). John also states that there were two angels, who appeared to Mary Magdalene after Peter and John had left the tomb (see John 20:11-13).
3. The Apostles' Creed was an early statement of belief based on Christian theological understandings of the Gospel, the letters of the New Testament and the Old Testament. Reference to an early form of the Creed appears for the first time in a letter from the Council in Milan to Pope Siricius in AD 390. Tradition holds that the original Creed was jointly created by the apostles under the direction of the Holy Spirit, with each of the Twelve contributing one of the articles.

Sources

Henrietta C. Mears, *What the Bible Is All About,* "Understanding Matthew," "Understanding Mark," "Understanding Luke," "Understanding John," "Understanding Acts" (Ventura, CA: Regal, 2011), chapters 27-30.

Mears, *Highlights of Scripture Part Four: Words and Works of Jesus, Teacher's Book* (Los Angeles, CA: The Gospel Light Press, 1937).

THE KINGDOM NEAR

Jesus' Parables of the Kingdom (Matthew 13:1-52; Mark 4:1-20; Luke 8:4-15)

SESSION FOCUS

Jesus' proclamations of God's manifest presence
and kingdom on earth.

KEY VERSE TO MEMORIZE

The kingdom of heaven is like treasure hidden in a field. When a man found it,
he hid it again, and then in his joy went and sold all he had and bought that field.
MATTHEW 13:44

WEEKLY READING

DAY 1	Matthew 10; 13
DAY 2	Mark 4; 6
DAY 3	Luke 8–9
DAY 4	Luke 10; 13
DAY 5	Matthew 16:28–17:13; Mark 9; Luke 9

FOR LEADERS: SESSION AT A GLANCE

SESSION OUTLINE	60 MIN.	90 MIN.	WHAT YOU WILL DO
Getting started	10	15	Pray and worship
Main points of the chapter	25	35	Discuss Jesus' parables on the kingdom of God
Application and discussion	15	25	Discuss personal application questions
Looking ahead	5	5	Prepare for next week
Wrapping up	5	10	Close with prayer or song

The Purpose of Parables

Up to this point in this study, we have focused on the *deeds* of Jesus. Now we will begin to look at the *words* of Jesus—specifically, the *parables* of Jesus. The parables that Jesus told were the hallmark of His teaching. They were so intrinsic and integral to His purposes that it is impossible to separate them from His message.

WHAT IS A PARABLE?

A "parable" (Greek *parabole*) is a short story that incorporates everyday events to illustrate a spiritual principle. It typically involves a character facing a moral dilemma or making a questionable decision and then suffering the consequences. Jesus used parables to illustrate a parallel between some aspect of everyday life on earth and a greater spiritual truth in God's kingdom.

Parables are not fables, which—though they have a moral—depend on fanciful conventions (such as talking animals) to carry the story along. They are somewhat like allegorical stories, but not quite the same. An allegory is a story with many reference points between two aspects of life; and each facet of an allegory, whether obvious or obscure, can be exploited for significance. For this reason, it is said that an allegory can "walk on all fours." A parable, on the other hand, has the aim of getting a single, emotional (or spiritual) point across. A parable shouldn't be forced to "walk on all fours." Those hearing the parable are supposed to get the main point, examine themselves, and then apply that point to their lives.

THE DISTINCTIVENESS OF JESUS' PARABLES

Jesus didn't teach the way that many philosophers and religious figures do, using jargon that only experts can understand and incorporating difficult or abstract ideas into His message. Instead, most of the time He taught using simple, down-to-earth stories drawn from first-century rural Jewish culture, which made His teachings accessible to common people. He used parables to make important points, and they were instantly memorable. Even today, though we are vastly removed from Jesus' time and geography, once we've heard His parables, it's hard to forget them.

DISTRIBUTION OF THE PARABLES

Many of the parables that Jesus told can be found in all three of the Synoptic Gospels. These include the following:

PARABLE	MATTHEW	MARK	LUKE
The Parable of Salt	5:13	9:49-50	14:34-35
Lamp and the Lampstand	5:14-15	4:21	8:16
Friends of the Bridegroom	9:14-15	2:18-20	5:33-35
Patching an Old Garment	9:16	2:21	5:36
New Wine in New Wineskins	9:17	2:22	5:37-38
Plundering the Strong Man	12:22-30	3:22-27	11:14-23
The Sower and the Seed	13:1-23	4:1-20	8:4-15
The Mustard Seed	13:31-32	4:30-32 .	13:18-19
A Negative Spin on Yeast	16:5-12	8:14-21	12:1
The Fig Tree	21:18-19; 24:32-36	11:12-14,20-24; 13:28-31	13:6-9; 21:29-33
The Wicked Tenants	21:33-41,43-46	12:1-12	20:9-19
The Rejected Cornerstone	21:42	12:10	20:17
The Thief in the Night	24:42-44	13:33-37	12:39-40

Some of the parables are found only in the Gospels of Matthew and Luke:

PARABLE	MATTHEW	LUKE
Treasures in Heaven	6:19-21	12:33-34
The Lamp of the Body	6:22-23	11:34-36
Serving Two Masters	6:24	16:13
Birds of the Air; Lilies of the Field	6:25-34	12:22-32
The Narrow Door	7:13-14,22-23	13:22-30
Knowing Them by Their Fruits	7:15-23	6:43-46
Building on the Rock	7:24-27	6:47-49
A Positive Spin on Yeast	13:33	13:20-22
The Warning of the Sky	16:2-3	12:54-56
The Great Banquet	22:1-14	14:15-24

PARABLE (CONT'D)	MATTHEW	LUKE
The Lost Sheep	18:10-14	15:1-7
The Days of Noah	24:37-41	17:26-36
The Faithful and Wise Steward	24:45-51	12:42-48
Waiting for the Bridegroom	25:1-13	12:35-38
The Parable of the Talents	25:14-30	19:11-27

Some of the parables only found in Matthew include the Parable of the Weeds (13:24-30,36-43); the Hidden Treasure (13:44); the Pearl (13:45-46); the Net (14:47-50); the New Treasures and Old (13:51-52); the Unmerciful Servant (18:23-25); the Workers in the Vineyard (20:1-16); the Two Sons (21:28-32); and the Sheep and the Goats (25:31-45).

Some of the best loved of all Jesus' parables are only found in Luke: the Two Debtors (7:41-43); the Good Samaritan (10:30-37); the Friend at Midnight (11:5-8); the Snake and the Scorpion (11:11-13); the Rich Fool (12:16-21); the Unfinished Tower (14:28-30); the King Going to War (14:31-33); the Lost Coin (15:8-10); the Prodigal Son (15:11-32); the Shrewd Manager (16:1-12); the Rich Man and Lazarus (16:19-31); the Condescending Master (17:7-10); the Unjust Judge (18:2-8); the Persistent Widow (18:2-8); and the Pharisee and the Tax Collector (18:10-14).

Only one parable is found only in Mark: the Growing Seed (4:26-29). Interestingly, the Gospel of John doesn't contain any parables. Nonetheless, what John's Gospel lacks in parables it makes up for in pithy parable-like pronouncements. For in John we find that Jesus gave Himself many titles, including the Bread of Life (6:35,48); the Living Bread from Heaven, a reference to the miraculous provision of manna that God gave the Israelites when they were starving in the wilderness desert (6:41,51); the Light of the World (John 8:12-20; 9:5); the Gate (10:7,9); the Good Shepherd (10:11,14); the Resurrection and the Life (11:25); the Way, the Truth and the Life (14:6); and the True Vine (15:1).

Parables of the Kingdom

Throughout the ages, different people have categorized Jesus' parables in different ways. For the purposes of this study guide, we will divide them into six categories:

1. Parables of the kingdom of God
2. Parables of loss and redemption
3. Parables of love and forgiveness
4. Parables on prayer
5. Stand-alone parables (a catch-all category)
6. Parables on the urgency of the hour

The Kingdom in the Old Testament

The kingdom of God is a central theme in the Gospels. John the Baptist prepared the way for Jesus' coming with his call to repent for the kingdom was "at hand" (Matthew 3:2, *KJV*) or had "come near" (*NIV*). In making this statement, John was referencing a concept that was familiar to the Jewish people at the time based on concepts of the kingdom of God found in the Hebrew Scriptures.

In the Old Testament, the kingdom of God represented the faithful actions of the Lord as King on behalf of His people. As their ruler, He would bless and protect them (see Numbers 23:21; Deuteronomy 33:5). As the king over the heavens and the earth, He would decide which nation would be victorious and which would be subject to its enemies (see 1 Kings 22:15-23; Psalms 2; 60; 83; 103:19). Men and women had to be pure to enter into the presence of the heavenly King (see Isaiah 6:5), and He appointed representatives to reign over His people on earth in order to establish His righteousness and justice. David and Solomon were two such representatives (see 1 Chronicles 29:11-12,23).

The kingdom of God also incorporated aspects of worship. In Exodus 19:5-6, the Lord told the Israelites that if they walked in obedience to Him, He would make them into "a kingdom of priests" who would usher the nations into His presence. In the book of Daniel, the prophet receives a vision in which he sees the Lord giving His kingdom authority to the Messianic "Son of Man," who will be worshiped by all nations (see Daniel 7:13-14,18,27). God's people, "the holy people of the Most High," would receive the Kingdom authority of the Lord and His Messiah so that "all rulers [would] worship and obey him" (Daniel 7:27).

During the Intertestamental Period (516 BC–AD 70), the Jews ascribed to the Lord kingly roles as judge, protector, defender and caring shepherd of His people. God showed Himself as king in mighty acts of war, in acts of righteousness and justice to maintain His law, and in gentle and compassionate acts that revealed Him as a shepherd caring for His flock.[1]

THE KINGDOM IN THE NEW TESTAMENT

Jesus represented the arrival of God's kingdom into this world and the initiation of God's rule in His people's lives through the Holy Spirit. Due to Old Testament prophecies about the Messiah vanquishing God's enemies and establishing peace and justice in the earth, the Jews associated the kingdom of God with the end of history or the end of the world as they knew it (see Luke 19:11). However, Jesus showed that the Kingdom was something much different. Rather than centering on military might, Jesus taught that the Kingdom centered on loving God with every part of their being and loving their neighbors as themselves (see Mark 12:30-34). Those who wanted to be a part of God's kingdom turned away from evil and obeyed God's will, for as Paul would later state, "wrongdoers will not inherit the kingdom of God" (1 Corinthians 6:9).

Jesus revealed that one enters into this kingdom of God through childlike and guileless faith (see Mark 10:15) and by being reborn through the power of God's Spirit (see John 3:5). In John 17:21, He told the Pharisees that the Kingdom was "within" them. The Early Church Fathers understood this to mean that the kingdom of God resides within people's hearts. They are reborn by God's Spirit, and the Spirit actively dwells within them, empowering them to walk in righteousness, peace and joy (see Romans 14:17; Galatians 4:6; Ephesians 3:17; Colossians 1:27).

In Matthew 10:1-8, when Jesus began His ministry, He sent out His disciples to heal people's diseases and deliver them from demonic spirits, telling them to proclaim that "the kingdom of heaven has come near." We find many other instances throughout the Gospels where the Kingdom is manifest through such miraculous healings and deliverances, all of which are accomplished through the power of the Holy Spirit (see Matthew 10:1,7-8; 12:28; 28:20; Luke 9:1-2; 10:1,9; 11:20). Later, the apostle Paul would affirm that the kingdom of God is not manifested in words only but by the power of the Holy Spirit through signs, wonders and healings (see Romans 15:18-19; 1 Corinthians 4:20). Through these miraculous events God was breaking into this world, making His presence known and felt by people in undeniable ways.

GOD AS "KING" OF HIS KINGDOM

In Jesus' teaching, the terms "the kingdom of God," "the kingdom of heaven" and "the kingdom" are interchangeable. (Matthew prefers the phrase "the kingdom of heaven," while Mark, Luke and John use "the kingdom of God" exclusively.) In this way, we see that "the kingdom" itself is a mini-parable, for Jesus calls us to see earthly kings and kingdoms (ignoring, for the moment, all of the self-serving and deceitful aspects of human kings and their kingdoms) as a picture of the greater spiritual reality of God as the royal ruler of His universe. His sovereignty compels us to give our worship and allegiance to Him and to Him alone.

God, as the sovereign ruler of His universe, is thus portrayed as a "king." However, it is a mistake to think of God as being either male or female, because this is not what Scripture teaches. Genesis 1:26-27 says that God made man "in His image." What is God's image? Both "male and female." God is beyond biology and gender.

This biblical understanding of the one true God is vastly different from the pagan perceptions of their gods. Pagan religions had an explicit tone of sexuality about them—the masculine gods almost always had feminine consorts. However, the God of the Bible does not need a feminine consort to balance the masculine side. The Bible even contains some feminine metaphors for God. The psalmists spoke of taking shelter in the shadow of God's wings, just as a chick would take shelter in its mother's wings (see Psalms 17:8; 36:7; 57:1; 61:4; 63:7; 91:4). Like a mother, God cannot forget His people (see Isaiah 49:15; 66:13). Jesus also likened Himself to a hen gathering her chicks (see Matthew 23:37).

Even so, God has chosen to reveal Himself primarily in masculine metaphors (such as "Father," "Son" and "King"). Jesus Himself called God "Father," "My Father" and "My heavenly Father." These metaphors maintain the distinctiveness of the God of the Bible over and against the pagan gods and goddesses. It also shows us that if it was okay for Jesus to call God "Father" and to rejoice in God's "King"-dom, then it is okay for us to do so as well.

The Sower and the Seed

In Matthew 13, we find the most important extended passage in the Bible on the kingdom of God. In this chapter, Christ gives eight parables in sequence to explain different aspects of the kingdom. He begins this message with the planting of the gospel message in the world and ends with the coming "harvest" at the end of this age.

On this particular occasion, Jesus was sitting in a boat at the north end of the Sea of Galilee. Many small creeks and inlets provided places for a boat to easily ride within a few feet of the shore. The smooth boulders located near the shoreline would have invited people to come and sit down and listen to Jesus' teachings. The crowd might have even positioned themselves on both sides of the boat or in front of it.

As Jesus sat there in the boat, perhaps He spied in the background a sower at work in the fields that overlooked the lake. Let's stop for a moment and think about that farmer and his farm. If you could have visited that field at harvest time, you would have found the owner, his wife and his children (and perhaps even hired helpers) cutting the wheat or barley stalks by hand with curved sickles. They would have tied the stalks into bundles to make them ready for threshing.

FOUR TYPES OF SOIL

The fields had four types of ground. The first type was ground near a path. In Jesus' day, narrow footpaths often crisscrossed the fields, and travelers of all sorts—on foot, donkey or horse—would use them to get from one place to the next. Jesus, the disciples and all of Jesus' hearers would have traveled over such paths many times, and they knew that if a sower scattered grain near such a path, he would be almost sure to drop a few grains there. Lying in plain sight of hungry birds, these seeds would soon be eaten. A second type of ground, typically found on the edges of the field, was often pitifully poor and thin. Stalks of grain trying to grow in this rocky ground had a rough time of it under the scorching sun. A third type of ground consisted of neglected areas where thorn bushes and thistles would grow to considerable size. While the soil was good, it needed some cultivation! Finally, the fourth type of ground consisted of good soil, where a single seed could produce a vigorous, tall stalk with a nice head of new grain.

FOUR TYPES OF HEARERS

Christ took this familiar scene and constructed a parable around it to communicate an important message to His listeners. In Matthew 13:18-23, He explained that the *field* represented the *world*. The *seed* the sowers planted was the *Word of God*. The *sowers* themselves were the *servants of God*, and the *soil* represented the hearts of the listeners on which the *Word of God* fell.

Jesus explained that there are four different types of hearers (or "soil"). Those in the first group (the soil near the path) hear the Word, but it goes in one ear and out the other. They do not give it a chance to penetrate the surface of their hearts, so the Word never has a chance to grow in them. It just lies on the surface, ready to be snatched away by the devil. Because of this, it is of no benefit to them.

Those in the second group (the rocky ground) are easily swayed and have no persistence. They hear the Word, but because they don't allow it to sink into their hearts, when troubles or persecution come their way they quickly fall away. Agriculturalists have learned that the care of the soil in which a seed grows is actually more important than the soil itself. The desert can be made to bloom with proper irrigation and enough fertilizer. Many soils have been treated and made to bring forth wonderful crops.

Those in the third group (the thorny ground) represent hearers who allow worries and the things of this world (the thorns) to get in the way of receiving God's Word. Thorns are bad because they choke the seed, and God says this choking can come about as a result of either poverty or riches. Because of this, we need to be wary of the "worries of this life," which afflict those with great need, and "the deceitfulness of wealth" (Mark 4:19), which afflicts those at the other end of the spectrum, for such things "choke the word, making it unfruitful."

Sometimes our companions, our work or our pleasures can also represent choking thorns and can cause unfruitfulness in our lives. We cannot have "two bests" in our lives—our best effort and our love cannot be divided. For this reason, we must clear out anything that takes our time and care away from our fellowship with God or distracts us from His purpose. We have to simply hack those things away!

Those in the final group (the good ground) are the ones who hear the Word, allow it to take root in their hearts, and produce a harvest for the Lord. The sign of a good garden, as we all know, is growth. Those who accept God's Word and cultivate it in their hearts and minds allow this type of growth in their lives. They live a life "worthy of the Lord and please him in every way: bearing fruit in every good work, growing in the knowledge of God" (Colossians 1:10).

BRINGING FORTH FRUIT

Here's a bit of a parable from our own country that illustrates how God works on the "soil" in our lives. Many years ago, some farmers in New England grew tired of their rocky soil, so they deserted their farms and allowed the land to fall into disrepair. Where plows once had worked the land, rocks and weeds now prevailed. The apple trees became stunted and broken, and the berry bushes overgrown. How differently God deals with His farms! He keeps working with us, overturning and seeding down, clearing away the rubbish, until by and by a farm that once seemed hopeless begins to bear fruit again. When these same New England farms were later taken over by undiscouraged people, the land revived and once again produced good crops.

God can use what seems like even the smallest seed to produce an abundant harvest. One time, a farmer in Connecticut found a small potato in his pocket as he came in from the field. Passing it to his 12-year-old boy, he said, "Here, plant that and I'll let you have all the land you need to raise it until you are of age." The boy cut the potato into as many pieces as it had eyes and planted it. At the end of the first year, he took the potatoes that had been produced and replanted the entire crop. By the end of the fourth year, the boy's harvest amounted to 400 bushels. The farmer, seeing that his boy's planting would soon entirely cover his land, asked his son to release him from his bargain.

If the idea of receiving this kind of return appeals to you, know that you can have it if you allow God's Word to take root in your life. As Jesus told His disciples, "The knowledge of the secrets of the kingdom of heaven has been given to you. . . . Whoever has will be given more, and they will have an abundance" (Matthew 13:11). However, note that while the farmer's inanimate ground is not responsible for itself, you *are* responsible for yourself. You have a responsibility to take the seed in deep, hold it fast, and give it a fair chance. When you do, you will find that it will bring forth fruit.

Other Parables of the Kingdom

The other parables of the kingdom that Jesus told in Matthew 13 include the Parable of the Weeds (13:24-30,36-43), the Parable of the Mustard Seed (13:31-32), the Parable of the Yeast (13:33), the Parable of the Hidden Treasure (13:44), the Parable of the Pearl (13:45-46), the Parable of the Net (13:47-50), and the Parable of the New Treasures and Old (13:52).

THE PARABLE OF THE WEEDS
In this parable, an enemy sows weeds ("tares" in the *KJV*) in a field along with the good grain. The master of the field knows that uprooting the weeds would ruin the good grain, so he tells his servants to let them ripen together and then separate them at harvest time. Later, Jesus explains that the good seed represents the people of His kingdom, the weeds represent

the people of the evil one, and that the harvest represents the end of the age. At that time, the angels will gather the grain and throw the weeds "into the blazing furnace, where there will be weeping and gnashing of teeth" (13:42). Two implications for this parable are that (1) God alone is competent to judge who is and who is not a true believer, and (2) we are not required or expected to seek absolute purity in the Church or think that church membership corresponds to being "in" the kingdom of God.

The Parables of the Mustard Seed and the Yeast

In the Parable of the Mustard Seed, Jesus made the point that God is so powerful that only a little amount of faith in Him is needed to see big results (see also Mark 4:30-32). He immediately followed this with the Parable of the Yeast, putting a positive spin on yeast ("leaven" in the *KJV*) by showing how it is added to bread to cause the whole loaf to rise—which is a good thing. Later, Jesus put a negative spin on yeast, warning the disciples to be on guard "against the yeast of the Pharisees and Sadducees" (Matthew 16:6). In this instance, the yeast is a symbol for hypocrisy (see Matthew 15:5-12; Mark 8:14-21; Luke 12:1).

The Parables of the Hidden Treasure and the Pearl

In these parables, a person finds something of inestimable worth (a hidden treasure and a pearl) and sells everything he has to obtain it. This parable has troubled some who thought it might indicate that salvation could be bought; however, this conclusion would go directly against Jesus' intent. Rather, this parable is consistent with Jesus' other teachings: to put God's kingdom first in one's life.

The Parable of the Net

In this parable, fishermen rake in a big catch and then separate the good fish from the bad. Jesus says that this is how it will be at the end of the age, when the angels will separate the wicked from the righteous. The angels will throw the wicked "into the blazing furnace, where there will be weeping and gnashing of teeth" (13:50). This is similar to the point Jesus was making in the Parable of the Weeds.

The Parable of the New Treasures and Old

In this concluding parable, Jesus states that "every teacher of the law who has become a disciple in the kingdom of heaven is like the owner of a

house who brings out of his storeroom new treasures as well as old"
(13:52). This parable has two dimensions: (1) an affirmation toward the
past (the Old Testament and the old covenant it represents), and (2) an affirmation toward the future (the New Testament, the Church, and the new
covenant they represent).

QUESTIONS FOR PERSONAL APPLICATION AND DISCUSSION

How is a parable different from a fable? How is it different from an allegory?

_____

_____

_____

_____

What was unique about the parables that Jesus told? Why did He often
choose to communicate His message to His listeners through parables?

_____

_____

_____

_____

_____

What was the Jewish people's expectation of "the kingdom of God"? In what
ways did Jesus' interpretation of the Kingdom challenge their mindset?

_____

_____

_____

_____

_____

Think about the Parable of the Sower that we studied in this session. What
type of people represent the soil near the footpath? What happens when
the seed of the Word of God is placed into their lives?

_____

_____

_____

_____

What is characteristic of the people who represent the rocky ground? What is the real reason they quit when troubles and persecution come their way?

_____

_____

_____

_____

_____

Someone once said, "Interest will begin a hard work. Grit will continue it. But only love makes a man endure to the end." What makes a person continue to do difficult things for the Master?

_____

_____

_____

_____

_____

What type of people represent the soil occupied by thorns and thistles? How can you root out the weeds in your life that choke the good seed?

_____

_____

_____

_____

_____

How have you nurtured the seed God has planted within you? What type of fruit is your life producing as a result of God sowing that seed?

_____

_____

_____

_____

Perhaps your life is more like the rocky or thorny ground. If so, what can you start doing now to begin moving toward becoming good soil?

_____

_____

_____

Read Isaiah 55:1-13. What are the actions and attitude that the prophet calls the people to adopt that make up living in the kingdom of God? What is the role of the Word of God in this framework?

_____

_____

_____

_____

_____

_____

What is the connection between God's kingdom and this present life (see Matthew 7:21-23; 12:28; Mark 12:30-34; Romans 14:17). What is the connection between God's kingdom and the next life (see Matthew 25:31-46)?

_____

_____

_____

_____

_____

_____

What is the connection between God's kingdom and wanting to see other people all across the globe have a chance to experience the kingdom of God and respond to the gospel of Jesus Christ (see Exodus 19:5-6; Matthew 28:18-20; Acts 1:8; Romans 15:18-19)?

_____

_____

_____

_____

_____

_____

Note

1. M. Brettler, *God Is King: Understanding an Israelite Metaphor* (Sheffield, UK: Sheffield Academic Press, 1990); W. O. McCready and A. Reinhartz, *Common Judaism: Explorations in Second-Temple Judaism* (Minneapolis, MN: Fortress Press, 2008), p. 136.

Source

Henrietta C. Mears, *Highlights of Scripture Part 3: Christ in My Everyday Life and Parables of Jesus, Teacher's Book* (Hollywood, CA: The Gospel Light Press, 1937), pp. 57-65, "The Sower and His Seed."

LOST AND FOUND

Jesus' Parables on Loss and Hope (Luke 15:1-32)

Jesus seeks out and saves the lost.

For this son of mine was dead and is alive again; he was lost and is found.
LUKE 15:24

DAY 1	Luke 15
DAY 2	Deuteronomy 30:15-20
DAY 3	Galatians 5:19-26; 1 John 3:1-24
DAY 4	Romans 8:1-18
DAY 5	Psalm 103:1-18

SESSION OUTLINE	60 MIN.	90 MIN.	WHAT YOU WILL DO
Getting started	10	15	Pray and worship
Main points of the chapter	25	35	Discuss Jesus' parables on loss and hope
Application and discussion	15	25	Discuss personal application questions
Looking ahead	5	5	Prepare for next week
Wrapping up	5	10	Close with prayer or song

Parables of Loss and Redemption

In 1719, Daniel Dafoe, an English writer, journalist and pamphleteer, published what was probably his best-known work, *Robinson Crusoe*. This novel purported to be an autobiography of a man marooned on an island, as can be discerned from its original long title: *The Life and Strange Surprizing Adventures of Robinson Crusoe, of York, Mariner: Who Lived Eight and Twenty Years, all Alone in an Un-inhabited Island on the Coast of America, Near the Mouth of the Great River of Oroonoque; Having Been Cast on Shore by Shipwreck, Wherein all the Men Perished but Himself. With an Account How He Was at Last as Strangely Deliver'd by Pyrates.*

Dafoe's book was an immediate success, and it has since gone through many printings, translations and spin-offs. Among these were *The Swiss Family Robinson* (1812), a German novel, Hollywood movie and TV series; *Robinson Crusoe on Mars* (1964), a science-fiction movie; *Lost in Space* (1965), a humorous science-fiction TV series; the films *Castaway* (1986) and *Cast Away* (2000); and the TV series *Lost*. We just can't seem to get enough of this story.

A UNIVERSAL HUMAN EXPERIENCE

Perhaps this is because *Robinson Crusoe* resonates with the universal human experience of loss. We lose our keys and other things more valuable. We lose friends. We lose loved ones. We lose our bearings and our direction. We lose our way. We lose our moral compass. Potentially, in chasing after things we want in life, we can even lose our own souls (see Matthew 16:26; Mark 8:36).

But what can be lost can also be found. To this end, Jesus' parables on loss and redemption answer to the ache that we all feel at times due to missed opportunities, regret about actions taken (or not taken), the severe separation of death, and the feeling of being lost spiritually. These parables—the Lost Sheep (Luke 15:1-7; Matthew 18:10-14), the Lost Coin (Luke 15:8-10), and the Lost Son (Luke 15:11-32)—are all infused with a message of tremendous hope.

JESUS' UNSAVORY COMPANY

Wherever Jesus went, He caused quite a stir. On this occasion, as Luke reports, "the tax collectors and sinners were all gathering around to hear Jesus" (Luke 15:1). The tax collectors represented those who sought after money, while the sinners represented those who didn't care as much about God's law or respectability. Each of these groups felt welcome around Jesus, and they wanted to hear Him teach.

To a religious Jew in Jesus' time, tax collectors and sinners belonged in the category of "infidels." Yet these were the very people with whom Jesus chose to hang out. Of course, the Pharisees and teachers of the law had a problem with His choice. They had kept themselves pure (and aloof) from the unclean riff-raff, but now here was Jesus spending time with them and even eating with them. What was He doing? What was He thinking?

Jesus knew this religious mindset well. He knew exactly what was bothering the Pharisees and teachers of the law. So He told them three stories to get them off their religious high horses and to realize what was really important in life. In the process, He also communicated a message of love and redemption to the lost souls who had gathered to hear Him speak.

The Lost Sheep

The first story that Jesus told on this occasion was the Parable of the Lost Sheep. In this story, a man who had 100 sheep discovered that one is missing. Not wanting to suffer the loss of any of his flock, he left the other 99 to go in search of that one missing sheep. Later, when he found it, the man rejoiced, put it on his shoulders and carried it home, where he called all of his friends together to tell them the good news.

At the conclusion of the parable, Jesus slyly said, "I tell you that in the same way there will be more rejoicing in heaven over one sinner who repents than over ninety-nine righteous persons who do not need to repent" (Luke 15:7). The lessons here couldn't be clearer: (1) sinners are "lost sheep" who need to be sought out and found; (2) we ought to care at least as much for sinners as lost sheep; (3) God and all the angels in heaven rejoice whenever a sinner repents; and (4) only those who know that they are sinners can repent. The final lesson to gain from the parable is two-edged: (1) righteous people don't need to repent, and (2) people who think they are righteous don't realize they need to repent.

Regarding this last point, we see how Jesus used this parable to get His listeners to engage in some self-examination and introspection. Elsewhere in Scripture, we find that no one can stand on his or her righteous merits before God—that all are sinners (see Psalms 14; 53; Isaiah 64:6). Using that scriptural perspective as a background, Jesus here forced the Pharisees and teachers of the law to make a choice: (1) congratulate themselves for being righteous, because they are religious (which, we have just seen, is absurd); or (2) admit that they, too, were sinners in need of repentance. And if they chose this last option—that they were sinners—then they couldn't keep looking down on the tax-gatherers and sinners, because they were in the same boat with them.

Isn't this an interesting approach? Jesus didn't condemn the non-religious or the religious group, but was content to leave things open-ended. The tax collectors and sinners understood that God loved them and would accept them if they chose to repent and turn to Him. The religious folks were free to keep on deceiving themselves into thinking they were better than others—or they, too, could repent and turn to God.

In John 10:14-16, Jesus said, "I am the good shepherd; I know my sheep and my sheep know me—just as the Father knows me and I know the Father. . . . I have other sheep that are not of this sheep pen. I must bring them also. They too will listen to my voice, and there shall be one flock and one shepherd." Isn't it incredible to know that Jesus is actively seeking out all those who are lost to bring them into His fold? All of heaven watches and celebrates whenever someone turns his or her life over to Christ!

The Lost Coin

Jesus followed up the first parable with a second. In this one, a woman had 10 silver coins but lost one. To find it, she turned the house upside-down, searching every nook and cranny for it. (The house gets a thorough cleaning!) When she finally finds the lost coin, she has the same reaction as the man who found the lost sheep. She rejoices with her friends.

In this parable, the inanimate coin represents a sinner who repents, and the woman's actions emphasize the act of God's *searching* for the lost even more. If you're good at sheep calling, you might be able to call a sheep and allow it to find you. Not so with a coin—all of the effort is on the part of the searcher. To God, every human being has intrinsic value. He will turn things upside down to find the one who is lost.

Jesus ended this parable the same way as the first: "I tell you, there is rejoicing in the presence of the angels of God over one sinner who repents" (15:10). While the earth raises its monuments and has its celebrations when humans do great things, God has His celebrations when the sinner, in failure and disgrace, comes back home to Him. From these two parables, we see that Jesus is truly elated wherever and whenever sinners repent and return to the Father.

The Lost Son

Jesus followed up the second parable with a third. This time, the story revolved around a lost son. Unlike the other two parables, this one contained three major characters. The first character was the father, who exhibited great patience with both of his sons and was eager to have fellowship with them. The second character, in the title role, was the younger son who chose to go away from home and seek out the pleasures of the world. The third character was the faithful older son, who felt slighted when his father welcomed back his prodigal brother.

In the Parable of the Lost Son, Jesus added a personal dimension to His stories of loss and redemption. While sheep and coins have little choice in the matter of being found, a lost human being is altogether different. For better or worse, each of us makes choices. We can't blame others, or God, or circumstances, for blocking our pathway to righteous living and peace. At any point, we can choose to respond to God's amazing grace.

A TYPICAL JEWISH HOME AT THE TIME OF JESUS

To better understand this parable, we need to imagine the conditions of family life in this home that Luke describes. The more specific the better, so let us imagine a house in Cana of Galilee, which would have been only four or five miles from our Lord's home in Nazareth, on the road to Capernaum.

As we approach the house, we see that a six-foot-high stone wall surrounds the structure. Stepping through the entrance, we enter into its sunny outdoor courtyard and stand on bare ground, trodden down hard by many feet. A two-story house rises directly before us. Barn doors on the ground level of the courtyard lead to stables. A stone staircase leads up to the second floor rooms where the family lives. Two small window holes permit all the sunlight that the rooms have. (This may explain the inconvenient darkness in the Parable of the Lost Coin in Luke 15:8.)

The family spends most of the waking hours out in the courtyard. Here, the women work and the children play. A half dozen women and girls are currently busy with various tasks. Some are washing clothes in big shallow basins set on the ground, while others are taking care of the babies. Nearby, a young man is standing by his herd of goats.

THE PATRIARCH AND THE INHERITANCE

Coming down the stone stairs, with an air of dignified authority, is the evident head of the household. He is gray-bearded, clad in a long robe of striped woolen material, and has a turban wrapped about his head. This man is the father of the young man and the father-in-law of the young women. His other sons must be out in the fields, or at market, attending to the business affairs of this extended family.

In this culture, it is not uncommon for grown-up sons to remain under their father's roof and authority even while their own little children are growing up. At the father's death, the property would be divided among the sons. According to the law of the time, if there were only two brothers, the elder would get two-thirds of the inheritance and the younger would get one-third.

UNDERLYING CONFLICTS

The Parable of the Lost Son is often called the Parable of the Prodigal Son. The word "prodigal" means extravagantly wasteful, which suggests that the central conflict might be about fiscal irresponsibility. However, the biggest conflict running through this story is that the younger son is not right with his father. He thinks he knows it all, and his father can't teach him anything.

The son is also stubborn and self-willed—he wants his own way. Complicating matters is the coming-of-age angle. He desperately wants to see something of the great world. It's hard to fault him for having this attitude. After all, if there were no restlessness in youth, there would be no progress.

DIGGING HIMSELF INTO A HOLE

Yet another conflict running through the story is that the younger son wants his freedom, but to enjoy that freedom, he needs somebody else's money. So he makes some choices. First, he chooses to ask his father for his portion of his inheritance—*before* his father dies. Second, he chooses to go to a faraway country, essentially cutting himself off from his family. Third, he chooses to eat, drink and be merry—to enjoy wine, women and song. Fourth, he chooses to squander his inheritance on high living and all the perks that go with conspicuous spending.

As long as the money lasts, everything is wonderful for the younger son. But then his house of cards comes falling down. One day he completely runs out of money, and at the same time a severe famine hits the land. The younger son looks around for his so-called friends, but they turn out to be fair-weather companions. It doesn't take him long to realize that he will have to fend for himself.

The younger son looks around and can't find any decent employment, so he ends up working for a pig farmer. He is paid so poorly that in order to avoid starvation he has to eat pig food—an ironic blow for someone who is Jewish and whose cultural tradition is to avoid anything having to do with pork. He's at the end of his rope. This son, the beloved son of his father, has thrown away his privileges and inheritance and has brought shame on his family.

The Wising Up

Now comes the climax of the younger son's story. He is suffering acutely. "He longed to fill his stomach with the pods that the pigs were eating, but no one gave him anything" (Luke 15:16). The fact that no one would help him is a testament to how low he had fallen—even the pigs were more valuable than he. However, while suffering is painful, even self-induced suffering often has an important place in God's purposes. In this case, the son's suffering did its work well and caused him to start thinking about what his life was like now as compared to what it used to be like when he was back home.

The son had to decide whether to return home. That choice to return was not forced—it was just as free as any of the other choices he had made. Nobody could repent for him, not even his father. Ultimately, the Bible states that he did come to his senses, saying to himself, "How many of my father's hired servants have food to spare, and here I am starving to death! I will set out and go back to my father" (Luke 15:17-18). He had been beside himself; now he came to himself.

Repenting Takes Guts

In the story, the younger son went through three steps of repentance. First, his suffering brought him to a place where he recognized his true condition. Second, he gained an accurate perspective of his sin. Third, he humbled himself and determined to return to his father. It takes courage to repent.

Note that one's motives for returning home to God do not have to be completely noble. In the younger son's case, with his realization that the hired men who worked for his father had enough food while he was starving, there seems to have been a twinge of self-interest and self-preservation involved. At any rate, he made a plan: "I will set out and go back to my father and say to him: Father, I have sinned against heaven and against you. I am no longer worthy to be called your son; make me like one of your hired servants" (Luke 15:18-19). He was willing to come back as a hired hand.

ONCE LOST, NOW FOUND

So the lost son set off on his return journey. Luke doesn't tell us how long the journey took, but when he was still quite a ways off from the homestead, the noble father, who had kept an eye on the horizon waiting for this day, spied his son. Filled with emotion, he *ran* to his wayward son (something a man in Middle Eastern culture never did) and embraced him. This is one of the high moments of the Bible, illustrating the great relief and joy that come with reunion, reconciliation and renewal of fellowship—the same kind of celebration that Jesus had just described in the earlier two parables. God yearns for us to return to Him.

The lost son gave his rehearsed speech, but the father immediately called together everyone in his house and all his hired workers to have a great feast. He said, "Quick! Bring the best robe and put it on him. Put a ring on his finger and sandals on his feet. Bring the fattened calf and kill it. Let's have a feast and celebrate. For this son of mine was dead and is alive again; he was lost and is found" (Luke 15:22-24).

AN EXERCISE IN MISSING THE POINT

The older brother thought very dimly of all the fuss. Why honor the good-for-nothing younger brother who was now crawling back home in disgrace? We might not have stood for it either, but that is heaven's way all the time.

An interesting twist to this part of the parable is how the attitude of the older brother might have played to the Pharisees and teachers of the law. The older brother reflects those who were complaining about Jesus welcoming the tax collectors and sinners (the "lost sheep" and "prodigals") who, in their eyes, didn't deserve all the fuss. Just as the older brother didn't want to acknowledge his younger brother as part of the family, the Pharisees and teachers of the law didn't want to be associated with the tax collectors and sinners—even when they were repenting! Like the older brother, they were positioning themselves as always having obeyed and served. In a way, then, this parable might have seemed as if Jesus were putting them down.

But then, Jesus puts these words on the lips of the father, who represents God in the parable: "My son . . . you are always with me, and everything I have is yours" (Luke 15:31). Like the elder son in the story, the Pharisees and teachers of the law did not realize the extent of the privileges that they had been given. Tenderly, Jesus reminded them that they, too, were beloved sons of God and that it was their duty to be glad when wanderers returned home.

The Chief Character of the Story

So, which of the characters is the most important in this parable? At first, it is easy to think that it is the prodigal son, but if we look carefully at the story, we find that the only reason so much is told about the son is to show that no sin is too bad for God to forgive. The main character is the father, and the message of the parable is to show God's love to sinners. What a father this prodigal had! What a God we have!

Questions for Personal Application and Discussion

When the tax collectors and sinners gathered around Jesus to hear Him speak, the Pharisees and teachers of the law said, "This man welcomes sinners and eats with them" (Luke 15:1). In what ways were the three parables that Jesus told directed to both groups? What was His message to each?

_____

_____

_____

_____

_____

Review the parable of the Lost Sheep in Luke 15:3-7 and the parallel account in Matthew 18:10-14. What does this story reveal about the way in which God seeks out the lost?

_____

_____

_____

_____

_____

What further insights did Jesus provide in the Parable of the Lost Coin about the ends to which the Father will go to find those who are lost? What does Jesus say happens when a sinner repents?

_____

_____

_____

_____

_____

Jesus never minimizes sin, nor does He ever act as if it would all come out all right in the end somehow. It will not come out right. As Paul wrote, "The wages of sin is death" (Romans 6:23). In light of this, why would the angels put on such a boisterous spectacle of rejoicing when a person turns away from sin and puts his or her trust in Christ?

_____

_____

_____

_____

_____

There are many instances in Scripture where God is referred to as a "Shepherd." Look up the following passages and write down what attribute of God is being portrayed.

SCRIPTURE	ATTRIBUTE OF GOD PORTRAYED
Psalm 23:1-3	
Isaiah 40:10-11	
Jeremiah 31:10	
Ezekiel 34:11-16	
Matthew 9:35-38	
John 10:11-16	
1 Peter 5:1-4	

The parable of the Lost Son is applicable to all of us because it presents us with two extremes: the younger son who goes to the limit in defiance and outward sin, and the older brother—a more cultured, respectable, decent fellow—who also happens to be quite self-centered. In your opinion, which set of sins is worse?

_____

_____

_____

_____

_____

How was the younger son "prodigal" (extravagantly wasteful)? In what ways have you been guilty of wasting your time, money, talents or opportunities that have been given to you as a share of God's treasure?

_____

_____

_____

_____

_____

What was the result of the son's decision to leave his father's home and follow his own desires? What in the parable indicates the depths to which the son had sunk in the esteem of others and in personal desperation for his condition?

_____

_____

_____

_____

_____

_____

Consider the following statement: "The beginning of all sin is an incapacity to find our fullest enjoyment in the presence of God." What does this mean to you?

_____

_____

_____

_____

_____

Charles Spurgeon once wrote, "We read [in the parable] that the father 'ran.' The compassion of God is followed by swift movements. He is slow to anger, but he is quick to bless. He does not take any time to consider how He shall show His love to penitent prodigals . . . God comes flying in the greatness of His compassion to help every poor penitent soul." What does this tell you about the character of God? How does this parable support the message Jesus was communicating in the parables of the Lost Sheep and the Lost Coin?

_____

_____

_____

_____

_____

_____

In what ways did the older son in the parable represent the Pharisees and the teachers of the law? What was Jesus' message to these groups? What is His message to us today?

_____

_____

_____

_____

_____

_____

_____

Source

Henrietta C. Mears, *Highlights of Scripture Part 3: Christ in My Everyday Life and Parables of Jesus, Teacher's Book* (Hollywood, CA: The Gospel Light Press, 1937), pp. 81-89, "The Prodigal Son."

A NEW WAY OF LOVING

Jesus' Parables on Love, Forgiveness and Reconciliation
(Matthew 18:21-35; Luke 7:36-50; 10:25-37)

SESSION FOCUS

Jesus' teachings on loving one another.

KEY VERSE TO MEMORIZE

But a Samaritan, as he traveled, came where the man was;
and when he saw him, he took pity on him.
LUKE 10:33

WEEKLY READING

DAY 1	Matthew 19:16-22; Luke 10:25-37
DAY 2	Matthew 22:34-40; Leviticus 19:18
DAY 3	Matthew 5:38-48
DAY 4	1 John 3:11-19; 1 Corinthians 13:1-13
DAY 5	Romans 15:1-13

FOR LEADERS: SESSION AT A GLANCE

SESSION OUTLINE	60 MIN.	90 MIN.	WHAT YOU WILL DO
Getting started	10	15	Pray and worship
Main points of the chapter	25	35	Discuss Jesus' parables on love, forgiveness and reconciliation
Application and discussion	15	25	Discuss personal application questions
Looking ahead	5	5	Prepare for next week
Wrapping up	5	10	Close with prayer or song

The Central Theme

If you had to boil down the central theme of Jesus' life and ministry on earth into just two or three words, those words might be "love and forgiveness." If you had to boil it all down into one word, a strong contender would be "reconciliation."

Reconciliation is relationship-repair. It is bringing back together that which had been wrecked, ruined or thought beyond repair. This message drives the gospel story. It is the animating motivation for God the Father sending God the Son to earth to redeem us. It is God the Holy Spirit's silent working behind the scenes to bring peace and reconciliation between Jews and Gentiles (see Ephesians 2:14-18) and to bring all things under Christ through His shed blood on the cross (see Colossians 1:19-20).

In the Sermon on the Mount, Jesus told His listeners that it was not good enough for them to just love those who loved them, but that they had to go the extra mile and love their enemies (see Matthew 5:43-48). Jesus even went so far as to say that if they did not forgive those who sinned against them, God would not forgive them (see Matthew 6:15; Mark 11:26). He said it was imperative for people in church to confront sin (see Matthew 18:15-20; Luke 17:3) and forgive each other, even up to "seventy times seven" times (Matthew 18:21-22; Luke 17:4, *KJV*).

Complementing Jesus' life mission and explicit teaching on love, forgiveness and reconciliation are the parables of the Two Debtors (Luke 7:40-50), the Unforgiving Servant (Matthew 18:23-35), and the Good Samaritan (Luke 10:29-37). We will examine each of these during this session.

The Two Debtors

The setting for the Parable of the Two Debtors told in Luke 7:36-50 is a dinner party for Jesus staged by Simon, one of the Pharisees. This might have been a somewhat strained encounter, as Jesus and the Pharisees didn't always get along. Jesus, however, never known to refuse an invitation, went and "reclined at table" with the Pharisee and his other guests (Luke 7:36).

The style of eating in those days was not like ours, where we sit on chairs at a table approximately 30 inches off the ground. Instead, diners sat on the floor or leaned back on one elbow, reaching up with the other hand to pick up food set on a low table. In this way, the guests' heads and shoulders were pointed toward the table, and their feet were pointed away from the table.

A SOCIALLY UNCOMFORTABLE MOMENT

While Jesus and the other diners were sitting in this position, a woman known for her bad reputation came up behind Christ and started weeping profusely on His feet, kissing them and wiping them with her long hair. As if that weren't enough, she then began to pour an expensive jar of perfume on His feet, the strong aroma filling the entire room and spilling out into the surrounding streets and alleyways (see Luke 7:36-69; similar stories are found in Matthew 26:6-13 and Mark 4:3-9).

This extravagantly choreographed and emotional demonstration would have caused a high degree of social awkwardness and embarrassment for the guests on several levels. First, men and women who were not related by birth or marriage were not supposed to have any physical contact with one another, much less such an intimate display as this. Second, this act would have caused intense curiosity and gossip on the part of the neighbors, who would certainly find out about it and gossip about it. There was no way the Pharisee would be able to keep the incident a secret. Third, everyone knew the woman's reputation, and this would have put the Pharisee's own reputation on the line (something Pharisees, who were known for their conservatism, really didn't like to have happen).

The chagrined Pharisee thought to himself, "If this man were a prophet, he would know who is touching him and what kind of woman she is—that she is a sinner" (Luke 7:39). Surely, if Jesus were a genuine prophet, He must have known that this woman had a low reputation. So why didn't Jesus put a stop to things right away? But then another possibility crossed his mind: Because Jesus had allowed the display, He must have been unaware that she was a loose woman and a sinner. A third possibility—that Jesus, as a prophet, knew that she was a sinner and still allowed her to carry on like that—was unthinkable.

As he was pondering this, Jesus called the Pharisee by his name, Simon, and said He had something to tell him.

A SIMPLE LITTLE STORY

Jesus then began to tell what is really a very simple and short story. In fact, it takes only two verses to tell: "Two men owed money to a certain moneylender. One owed him five hundred denarii, and the other fifty. Neither of them had the money to pay him back, so he forgave the debts of both" (Luke 7:41-42). Note that a *denarius* (plural *denarii*) is equivalent to the average day's pay for a day laborer (see Matthew 20:2).

Then Jesus asked Simon, "Now which of them will love him more?" Simon gave the only possible answer—"I suppose the one who had the bigger debt forgiven"—and Jesus complimented him on getting the right answer (7:42-43). Then Jesus pointed at the woman and, far from rebuking her for her impropriety, started heaping her with praise. He pointed out that she had shown Him much love, supplying in abundance much of the hospitality that would normally have been given to a guest of honor.

Then Jesus did three amazing things. First, He pronounced that her past sins, "which are many" (verse 47, *KJV*), were forgiven. In doing so, He dispelled any doubts that Simon and the other guests might have had about His awareness of her reputation. He also shocked them by ascribing to Himself something that only God could do—namely, forgive sins.

Second, Jesus identified the woman with the person in the parable who loved much because she had been forgiven much. "Whoever has been forgiven little loves little," He said, forcing the Pharisee and his guests to question their own attitudes (verse 47). If they had considered themselves morally superior to the woman, then they would have little for which to be forgiven, and therefore would love God "little."

Third, while the guests were still reeling from Jesus' first pronouncement that the woman's sins had been forgiven, He went a step further and pronounced her future salvation secure. "Your faith has saved you; go in peace," He said to her (verse 50). Jesus' new kind of forgiveness was not just for the "righteous" but also for everyone.

The Unforgiving Servant

The Parable of the Unforgiving Servant told in Matthew 18:21-35 begins with Peter asking Jesus how many times he is to forgive. There is a textual question about whether Jesus answered "seventy seven times" (*NIV*) or "seventy times seven" (*KJV*).[1] Either way, we are not to take the saying literally, as if forgiveness ends at 77 or 490 times. Jesus' intention is to indicate that putting offenses on a ledger and counting that high is absurd. In addition, it is helpful to know that Hebrew numbers often carry symbolic meanings. Seven is understood to be the number of completion and wholeness; thus, 77 or 490 would both indicate an infinite number of times.

After making this statement to Peter, Jesus then launches into the parable. A king wants to settle accounts with his servants. One servant is hopelessly in arrears, with no chance of ever paying the king back. So the king threatens to sell the man, his wife and his children into slavery and liquidate all his possessions in order to get something back on his invest-ment. When the servant begs the king to forgive him, the king mercifully forgives the unpayable debt.

However, the first servant then turns around and refuses to extend mercy to a fellow servant who owes him a small debt. He even has the fel-low servant thrown into debtors prison until he paid the amount. The first servant's ungratefulness and lack of mercy lead to a bad end. Word reaches the king of the first servant's deeds, and he calls the man back in to see him. "You wicked servant," the king says. "I canceled all that debt of yours because you begged me to. Shouldn't you have had mercy on your fellow servant just as I had on you?" (Matthew 18:32-33). The king hands him over to the jailors until he can pay back all that he owes.

Like the Parable of the Two Debtors, Jesus told this story so that His listeners would appreciate God's great mercy on them. However, this para-ble takes matters one step further, stating that in the same way we have received forgiveness and mercy from God's heart, we are to extend forgive-ness and mercy to others from our hearts.

The Good Samaritan

One day a legal scholar asked Jesus, "Teacher . . . what must I do to inherit eternal life?" (Luke 10:25). Some have suspected this expert was insincere in his question—that he, like other teachers of the law, was trying to trap Jesus. But there is no indication from the conversation that the man's attitude was overcritical or hostile. As an expert in the law of Moses, he simply wanted to know (in good faith) if Jesus' teachings were in accord with the Mosaic Law.

Christ met the lawyer on his own terms. He began the tutorial like any good teacher—by answering the question with a question. Jesus' question was one that the lawyer would have had no trouble answering. We can see from his answer that he knew the law well, quoting the two most impor-tant Scriptures in the Hebrew Bible: "Love the Lord your God with all your heart and with all your soul and with all your strength and with all your mind" (Deuteronomy 6:5) and "Love your neighbor as yourself" (Leviti-cus 19:18). These are exactly the same two verses Jesus Himself cited as the Greatest Commandment (see Matthew 22:37-39).

After the expert in the law had given this answer, Jesus said, "You have answered correctly. . . . Do this and you will live" (Luke 10:28). At this point, we would expect this little episode to end and the next to begin. But alas! Deep down, the lawyer knew—and Jesus knew, and everyone listening knew—that nobody keeps those two commandments. An awkward pause probably ensued.

A DEEP QUESTION

To fill in the silence and shift the topic, the lawyer posed the kind of question lawyers are good at: "And who is my neighbor?" (verse 29). This wasn't just an academic question; it is actually quite profound. On one level, it reached all the way back to one of the earliest chapters of the Bible when—immediately after Cain had murdered Abel—God asked Cain where his brother was. Cain answered, "How should I know? . . . Am I supposed to look after my brother?" (Genesis 4:9, *CEV*). Although the question comes from Cain the murderer, it's an extremely important question!

On another level, the lawyer's question brought up a whole body of Mosaic law concerning how the Israelites were to treat each other, along with the foreigners who aligned themselves with Israel. On still another level, it raised questions about how religious Jews were to act toward those in the community who weren't so religious (and, with that, issues of outward conformity to the law but inward rebellion, self-righteous attitudes and hypocrisy).

On yet still another level, the question brought up the complicated history between the Jewish people themselves (as God's Chosen People) and the Gentiles—the non-Jewish peoples whom the Jews considered outsiders, spiritually unclean and under God's judgment.

THE ORIGIN OF THE SAMARITANS

Finally, the question evoked the painful history of the Jews and the Samaritans. The short version of that story hearkens back to the days, 700 years earlier, when Israel was divided between the 10 tribes of the Northern Kingdom and the two tribes of the Southern Kingdom. In 722 BC by our calendar, the Assyrians conquered the Northern Kingdom. To prevent any uprisings or opposition to their rule, the Assyrians uprooted the conquered people from where they lived and settled them in other Assyrian-held lands. They knew that the remnant they placed in those lands would have to absorb the cultures of the other conquered peoples placed in that region. This policy resulted in a compliant populace, a lot of cultural intermingling, and cross-cultural marriage.

The 10 northern tribes disappeared from history. Except they didn't totally disappear. A remnant, located in Samaria and isolated from their spiritual cousins in the south, sought to preserve what they could of their culture and history. They held to the five books of Moses but rejected the later wisdom, literature and prophets of Israel. They also developed a slightly different set of rituals and venerated different places (see John 4:20-21).

The Jews generally suspected the Samaritans of spiritual and racial pollution, of mixing with Gentile religions, and of intermarriage with Gentile peoples. The Jewish religious authorities refused to let the Samaritans worship with them in Jerusalem or share in the rebuilding of the Temple after the time of captivity. So the Samaritans built their own temple on Mount Gerizim, thus becoming a rival religious sect on the margins of Judaism. The majority of Jewish people had a low opinion of the Samaritans, regarded them as half-breeds, and wanted to have as little to do with them as possible.

Today, about 700 Samaritans survive in two communities. (A general refusal to accept converts has led to the low population.) Half of them are located in the West Bank town of Nablus on Mount Gerizim, and the other half are located near Tel Aviv in Israel. The head of the community is the Samaritan High Priest, who is selected by age from the priestly family, and he resides on Mount Gerizim.

A TREACHEROUS ROAD

With this background in place, we can now examine the parable itself. A traveler was going down from Jerusalem to Jericho. Jerusalem was set on a hill, while Jericho was located down near the Dead Sea, approximately 1,200 feet below sea level. The road was steep, rocky and lonely, and bandits had hundreds of hiding places in which to lurk. They could rob a man and then conceal themselves in the rocks and never be found. This is what happened to the man: "he was attacked by robbers" (Luke 10:30). They took everything he had and left him for dead.

TWO WHO PASSED BY

A priest—who represented a good, upstanding, religious person in the community—was the first to come across the wounded man. We would expect a compassionate response from this person, but instead the man hurried by. Perhaps he was late for an important religious meeting. We don't know. Whatever his reasons, stopping to help the traveller just didn't fit into his schedule. Next came a Levite, who represented another example of a good, upstanding, religious person in the community. However, he too turned aside and walked quickly past.

ALONG COMES A NEIGHBOR

Soon, the suffering man heard the hoofs of a donkey. When the rider saw the man, he realized that he was in distress and stopped to help him. Even though this Samaritan didn't belong to the right "church," he took the time to help a fellow human being who was in deep trouble. He got off his donkey, gave the man some first aid, turned his mule into an ambulance, and carried the wounded man to an inn by the side of the road.[2]

The Samaritan took the wounded man into the inn and gave the innkeeper two denarii (remember that this would have been equivalent to two days' pay for a laborer). He said to the innkeeper, "Look after him . . . and when I return, I will reimburse you for any extra expense you may have" (Luke 10:35). In doing so, the Good Samaritan acted like a Christian.

How many times people who do not even profess to know Christ act more Christlike than those who are Christians! We must be careful how we act, for Christ is being judged by the spirit we show. We are His representatives. If we are mean and stingy and selfish, people will think this of Christ. If we are loving and kind, then they will love our Christ.

WHOSE NEIGHBOR AM I?

In the end, Jesus didn't answer the lawyer's question but rather asked another question: "Which of these three do you think was a neighbor to the man who fell into the hands of robbers?" (Luke 10:36). The main point is not who is our neighbor but to whom we can be a neighbor. Being a neighbor is not simply a matter of living next door to someone else—it's about loving and serving others.

Love finds neighbors. Love makes neighbors. A neighbor is not one who finds the mark of a neighbor in others but who possesses the marks of a neighbor within.

Many people on the highway of life have been robbed. Some have been robbed of health, some have been robbed of basic necessities, some have been robbed of money, and some have been robbed of the opportunity of education and training. Some are robbed spiritually and know nothing about the Lord.

Real-Life Applications

The gospel of forgiveness and reconciliation has both next-world applications (getting right with God, justification by faith, eternal salvation, getting into heaven) and hard-as-tacks, practical, this-world applications. We see these practical applications on a wider scale than just in personal relationships. For example, the American Civil War in 1861 (and the Civil Rights Movement 100 years later) was fought to advance the Christian principle of the equality of the races.

During the 1950s and 1960s, Catholic priests and nuns in Latin America began confronting the legacy of the Church's compliance with political power structures that had denied people's basic rights and had brutally oppressed the poor in those countries. These attempts at reconciliation often affected them on a personal level—by 1980, more than 50 priests had been killed for their activities, including an archbishop.

In 1994, the system of legal racial segregation known as apartheid was finally abolished in South Africa after nearly 50 years of enforcement. One year later, the government set up the Truth and Reconciliation Commission and offered amnesty to anyone who had committed crimes of racial hatred in exchange for telling the truth about what they did. In making this move, the government made the determination that forgiving those who had been a part of the former system and bringing them into reconciliation in the new system was more important than punishing them for their past offenses.

In recent years, we have also seen a movement toward healing America's wounds between Christian descendants of the First Peoples (Native Americans) and white beneficiaries of "Manifest Destiny." We also see initiatives by those same First Peoples groups encouraging reconciliation in other hot spots around the world, such as Northern Ireland, where hundreds of years of bad blood and murders between Catholics and Protestants had seemed to doom them to an unending cycle of violence. Since 1998, the two communities have now been working toward a lasting peace.

QUESTIONS FOR PERSONAL APPLICATION AND DISCUSSION

At the beginning of this session, we noted that love and forgiveness was a central theme of Jesus' life and ministry on earth. In the following table, write down some of Jesus' other teachings found in the Gospels on love and forgiveness.

PASSAGE	TEACHINGS ON LOVE/FORGIVENESS
Matthew 6:14	
Matthew 10:27	
Mark 11:25	
Luke 6:32	
John 13:34-35	
John 14:15	
John 15:13	

When Jesus was at the home of Simon the Pharisee and the woman began weeping profusely on His feet, the guests experienced a socially awkward moment. What factors caused them to feel uncomfortable? What tends to cause us to have awkward social moments?

_____

_____

_____

_____

_____

How did Jesus deal with these kinds of social pressures? What do you think helped Him keep His equilibrium in these situations? What can we learn from how He acted in uncomfortable social situations such as these?

_____

_____

_____

_____

_____

We are all tempted from time to time to conform to those around us—to please people instead of God—and for this reason we have scriptural warnings such as "bad company corrupts good character" (1 Corinthians 15:33) and "walk with the wise and become wise, for a companion of fools suffers harm" (Proverbs 13:20). However, we see in the Gospels that Jesus mingled with tax gatherers and sinners! How can we avoid cutting ourselves off from the kinds of people with whom Jesus mingled, but still avoid being influenced to fall into patterns of sin?

_____

_____

_____

_____

_____

What was the point of Jesus' Parable of the Unforgiving Servant as it related to Peter's question in Matthew 18:21?

_____

_____

_____

_____

_____

Sometimes the biggest hindrances to us showing compassion for others are religiously inspired. What examples did Jesus present of this in the Parable of the Good Samaritan? What examples of this do you see happening today?

_____

_____

_____

_____

_____

Luke 10:33 says, "But a Samaritan, as he traveled, came where the man was; and when he saw him, he took pity on him." How can you put yourself in the path of need?

_____

_____

_____

_____

_____

Throughout the Bible, we find many passages where God commands His people to treat those of other races with kindness and equality. Look up each of the passages in the following table and write down what it says about how we should treat other races.

SCRIPTURE	WHAT THIS SAYS ABOUT HOW TO TREAT PEOPLE OF OTHER RACES
Matthew 6:14	
Matthew 10:27	
Matthew 11:25	
Mark 11:25	
Luke 6:32	
John 13:34-35	
John 14:15	
John 15:13	

Look again at the Real-Life Applications section at the end of the chapter. Why are these kinds of initiatives important for the advancement of the gospel in our fractured world?

_____

_____

_____

_____

_____

Notes

1. In the original Greek, Christ's response (*hebdomekontakis hepta*) literally means "seventy times seven." However, the suffix added to seventy (*kis*) was used in two ways: (1) to refer to "times" as in a multiple (70 x 7), or (2) to refer to "times" as in a number of occurrences (forgive 70 times). Most scholars actually prefer "seventy-seven times" because of some rather complicated grammar associated with Peter's question.

2. The site of this inn is on the road down to Jericho today. It is the only place for miles around where a traveler can get water, and every passerby stops to get a drink.

Source

Henrietta C. Mears, *Highlights of Scripture Part 3: Christ in My Everyday Life and Parables of Jesus, Teacher's Book* (Hollywood, CA: The Gospel Light Press, 1937), pp. 66-72, "The Good Samaritan."

BETWEEN FRIENDS

Jesus' Parables on Prayer (Matthew 9:14-17; Mark 2:18-22; Luke 5:33-39; 11:5-13; 18:1-14

SESSION FOCUS

The importance of prayer in Jesus' life and ministry.

KEY VERSE TO MEMORIZE

If you then, though you are evil, know how to give good gifts to your children, how much more will your Father in heaven give the Holy Spirit to those who ask him!
LUKE 11:13

WEEKLY READING

Day 1	Proverbs 17:17; 18:24; John 15:12-16
Day 2	1 Samuel 18:1-5; Proverbs 27:9-10
Day 3	Hebrews 2:14-18; 4:14-16; Luke 5:33-39 (Matthew 9:14-17; Mark 2:18-20)
Day 4	Luke 11:1-13 (Matthew 6:9-13)
Day 5	Luke 18

FOR LEADERS: SESSION AT A GLANCE

SESSION OUTLINE	60 MIN.	90 MIN.	WHAT YOU WILL DO
Getting started	10	15	Pray and worship
Main points of the chapter	25	35	Discuss Jesus' parables on prayer
Application and discussion	15	25	Discuss personal application questions
Looking ahead	5	5	Prepare for next week
Wrapping up	5	10	Close with prayer or song

The Mystery of the Trinity

The topic of prayer immediately plunges us into the mystery of the Trinity. From all eternity, the one true God has existed as God the Father, God the Son and God the Holy Spirit—in perfect fellowship, communication, communion and glory. God is not a sterile entity, living in secluded isolation, but exists in relationship with Himself as love. As John simply stated, "God is love" (1 John 4:8).

It is for this reason that, as people created in God's image (see Genesis 1:27), we naturally yearn for a relationship with God. God intends for that relationship to be a genuine two-way relationship, not just one-way, as in that of a master and slave. Prayer is our method of communication with God. It begins with God the Father, is carried on by the Son, and is completed by the Holy Spirit. As Jesus acknowledged in John 5:30, "By myself I can do nothing; I judge only as I hear, and my judgment is just, for I seek not to please myself but him who sent me." It was God who initiated things, and Jesus acted on the Father's initiative. Jesus is our pattern, so we also should be taking our cues from the Father and praying His will back to Him.

When we pray in the name of Jesus, we are (as best we can) trying to pray as Jesus did, following the Father's initiatives. We pray through the Holy Spirit, who, when we don't even know how to pray, helps us "with groanings too deep for words" (Romans 8:26, *NASB*). Thus, we see that prayer is not about technique, or formulas, or having the right words—in fact, if we ever make it about those things, we're completely missing the point. So, what is prayer all about?

A Meditation on Friendship

From a biblical perspective, friendship is a "common grace." This is a type of grace people receive from God whether or not they are His followers. It is for everyone—such as a warm summer day, a beautiful sunset, a great meal, laughter and friends.

Companions are a gift from God. Each one of us should have friendships that we cultivate, and we should grow rich in them. While it is important to build such relationships in our youth—friendships established when we are young can grow richer in time—the truth is that we can make wonderful friends at any point in our life.

The worth of a true friend is beyond measure. We may have hundreds of acquaintances during our lives, but the number of true friends we will

have will be few and far between. When we find a true, staunch friend—
one who understands us and will stick with us under every circumstance—
then we are rich indeed.

Friendships stop at nothing except falsehood. A true friend desires nothing but the best for the other person. The good news is that every one of us can have this kind of a friend. As Scripture states, "There is a friend who sticks closer than a brother" (Proverbs 18:24). Jesus Christ is such a friend.

Friendship with Jesus

In John 15:15, Jesus told His disciples, "I no longer call you servants, because a servant does not know his master's business. Instead, I have called you friends, for everything that I learned from my Father I have made known to you." As the apostle Paul tells us in Philippians 2:1-11, no sacrifice was too great for Jesus to make for His friends. He laid aside His divine privileges and His station as King for them—and for us. It was a huge step down for His pure soul, but He did it. He is the greatest Friend the world has ever known. As the hymn so accurately states, *"What a Friend we have in Jesus, all our sins and griefs to bear! What a privilege to carry everything to God in prayer!"*

There was once a beautiful young girl who was a Christian. Although no other member of her family professed to be a follower of the Lord Jesus Christ, everyone marveled at her Christian life and the joy that she possessed. She wore a little locket constantly, and when she died at a young age, the family opened it, expecting to see the picture of some friend, or loved one, or even a lock of hair or other keepsake. But instead, all they discovered were these words: "Whom having not seen I love." Jesus Christ was real to her and the secret of her great joy. He was her constant companion.

Isn't it wonderful to think that Christ is not only our Savior but also our friend? The highest of all friendships is found in Jesus. Christ often took His disciples aside simply to enjoy them. What a scene it must have been to hear those friends enjoying each others' company, talking, laughing, joking and sharing each others' secrets.

Our Need for Friendship

A true friend sees the good in us that others miss. He or she knows our faults (but loves us anyway), believes in us, and brings out the best in us. Think of the disciple Peter. Christ saw strength in Peter that Peter could not yet see in himself (see Matthew 16:18-19). Love "believes all things" (1 Corinthians 13:7, *NASB*).

Christ's love believes in us even when we are unworthy and unreliable. "While we were still sinners, Christ died for us" (Romans 5:8). Having such a friend as Christ creates new possibilities in us. It breaks us and makes us. It never gives up on us. The friendship of Christ will carry us through to the end (see John 13:1).

We may be faithless, but He is ever faithful. We may grieve Him, but that has not made Him less of a friend. He is there still, just where He was before. His love is not "puppy love," infatuation, fake love or imitation love. It is real. "[His] love is as strong as death . . . it burns like blazing fire, like a mighty flame. Many waters cannot quench [it]; rivers cannot sweep it away" (Song of Solomon 8:6-7). It is because of this love that we can love others. "We love because he first loved us" (1 John 4:19).

So, how do we treat such a friendship as this? Do we take it for granted? Or do we value it and let it transform us?

Qualities of Friendship

Whether we are talking about friendship with Christ or another person, certain things must be happening in the relationship.

ENJOYMENT OF EACH OTHER'S COMPANY

First, you and the other person must truly enjoy one another's company. Friends *want* to spend time with each other. The presence of that person lights up your life, regardless of where you are or what you are doing. How many a Christian has been happy in a lonely dungeon because his or her great Friend was present there as well!

CONSIDERATION OF FEELINGS

Friends must be considerate of each other's feelings. You may admire and respect a person who is brave, witty or funny, but you will not want that person for a friend if he or she is inconsiderate of your feelings. David and Jonathan had that kind of considerate friendship (see 1 Samuel 18:1-5). No one can destroy such a fellowship.

TIME SPENT TOGETHER

Friends must spend time together. You need to be able to share what's going on in your life with the other person, and that person needs to be able to share what is going on in his or her life with you. Whether some great fortune befalls you or some terrible tragedy, you want your friend to know about it.

A LEVEL OF COMFORT

Friends need to feel comfortable to be themselves around each other. You can be silent, or silly, or serious without fear of embarrassment. You can speak your whole mind and heart and hold nothing back.

LOYALTY TO THE OTHER PERSON

Friends must be loyal. Someone has said that a friend is one who comes in when all the rest of the world has gone out. Does Jesus Christ live up to that expectation? He says, "Never will I leave you; never will I forsake you" (Hebrews 13:5).

STEADFAST COMMITMENT

Friends are steadfast. Think of the steadfast friendship that bound the disciples to Jesus. Although they all ran from the scene of the crucifixion (except for John), every one of them later laid down his life for Christ. Souls who were timid before Pentecost became bold as lions afterward. Their early vacillations were over-matched by Christ's steadfastness and loyalty to them. Of course, there was one sad exception—even Jesus' unmeasured love could not hold Judas fast. Think of how the Master's love inspired steadfast devotion to Him through all the subsequent centuries. How many millions have been inspired by His life, and love and example! How many martyrs have gladly given their lives for their faith![1]

RESPECT AND ACCEPTANCE

Real friends respect one another and are never ashamed of one another. You want to take that person with you and introduce him or her to others. You consider it a privilege to be known as that person's friend. If you are hesitant to mention that individual's name when you are with other friends, then that person is not actually a comrade of yours.

A DESIRE TO PUT THE OTHER PERSON ABOVE YOURSELF

Finally, friends do not take advantage of one another. Our lives will be filled with human friendships (or ought to be) and Jesus, our Friend, is the one who supplies those human friendships. Therefore, we need to be careful not to let selfishness mar our friendships. We shouldn't cherish friends only for what they are to us, nor should we think about what we mean to them.

We can't predict who our friends will turn out to be. When the pure Son of God took on flesh and became human, who could have predicted that His society, by and large, would not be with the high and mighty in "society"? Or that He would travel with a motley crew of fishermen, a tax collector, and a zealot? Or that He would befriend Pharisees, common people from all walks of life, and (horrors!) sinners?

Developing a True Friendship with Christ

As you look over all these qualifications of friendship and compare them to your current relationship with Christ, you might be thinking, *I wish I had such a Friend.* So, how do you develop such a fellowship? Here are some things to think about.

TRUST YOUR FRIEND IMPLICITLY

Have you put your absolute trust in the Lord Jesus Christ? Perhaps one of the reasons why so many people think following Jesus is hard is because they fail to understand the essential point about Christian faith: It is, at its core, a friendship with Jesus. There are thousands of fine people in our churches who have never realized this fact. They have a *religion about Jesus* instead of a *relationship with Jesus.*

CONFIDE IN YOUR FRIEND THOROUGHLY

Friendship does not mean knowing *about* a person. It means actually *knowing* that person. Each secret we hold back from a friend is a brick in a wall that separates us. There can be no wall of misunderstanding between friends. As the psalmist said, "Search me, God, and know my heart" (Psalm 139:23). We must open wide the door to our hearts to Jesus and yield ourselves to Him. We can tell Him our secrets and know that He will tell us His. Christ wants us to know what is in His heart.

SHARE COMMON INTERESTS

The Christian life is not merely about trying to be good or trying to avoid doing the wrong things. Rather, it is about seeking to have a deeper experience of fellowship with Christ. Christ is interested in the most common things of our lives. He is interested in everything we have to do, and He is ready to help us in all of it. He reveals Himself to us in the common tasks of the dullest day.

Some of the duties you will have to perform throughout your day will be irksome. However, if you accept these tasks cheerfully, Christ will reveal Himself to you as you do them. It's just like an earthly friend who comes and helps you out with something. You will do the same for him or her.

Christ told us to seek God's kingdom and His righteousness and we wouldn't have to worry about our basic human needs (see Matthew 6:33). But Christ won't come to you when you are avoiding your tasks and shirking your duties, or when you are discontented or fretting over your circumstances of life. He comes when you are doing your part and carrying your share of the load.

Parables on Prayer

As we discussed previously, in John's Gospel we find many titles for Jesus that represent parable-like pronouncements, and Jesus' theme of "the kingdom" was itself a mini-parable. The same can be said for friendship. John's Gospel is the most explicit about this when it states that Jesus chose us and appointed us so we "might go and bear fruit—fruit that will last" (John 15:16). This mini-parable is a foundational truth we need to understand as we begin to examine Jesus' parables on prayer and asking God for things.

THE FRIENDS OF THE BRIDEGROOM

The set-up for this parable (told in Matthew 9:14-15, Mark 2:18-20 and Luke 5:33-35) is that Jesus and His disciples were not acting the way some thought religious people should act—they were not being morose and serious and fasting and praying all the time. They asked Jesus why His disciples ate and drank and seemed to generally be enjoying themselves. Jesus answered by giving His critics three short word-pictures.

In the first of these, Jesus likened Himself to a bridegroom (you know, the really happy guy about to get married). He asked them why the groomsmen (the disciples) should fast when they were with the bridegroom. The image of "bridegroom" would have triggered certain associations among His Jewish listeners, such as the "Belover" and the "Beloved" in the Song of Solomon (see Song of Songs 6:3), or God's role of being the divine Husband of His people (see Isaiah 54:5). But it would have also raised some questions in their minds. What was Jesus really driving at?

To help them out, Jesus provided a domestic illustration. "No one sews a patch of unshrunk cloth on an old garment," He said. "Otherwise, the new piece will pull away from the old, making the tear worse." Shifting to winemaking, He added, "And no one pours new wine into old wineskins. Otherwise, the wine will burst the skins, and both the wine and the wineskins will be ruined. No, they pour new wine into new wineskins" (Mark 2:21-22; see also Matthew 9:16-17; Luke 5:36-39).

By using each of these illustrations, Jesus was indicating to the people that He came to bring something new—something that might not fit into their preconceived notions regarding prayer, fasting and many other things as well.

THE FRIEND AT MIDNIGHT

Prior to telling this parable, Jesus had just given His disciples instruction on a pattern for prayer that we now call the Lord's Prayer (see Luke 11:1-4). He followed this up with an amusing parable in which He asked His disciples to imagine that a friend arrived at their home late at night after a long journey, but they had no food to offer him. So they dropped by another friend's house unannounced and asked him to lend them three loaves of bread. At first the friend waved them off, saying, "Don't bother me. The door is already locked, and my children and I are in bed. I can't get up and give you anything." Eventually, however, the friend relents, gets up and gives them as much as they need (see Luke 11:5-8).

It is interesting that Jesus put God in the role of the sleepy friend who apparently didn't want to be bothered! However, that was not the point of the parable—far from it. The real point Jesus was making was that the disciples could approach God and expect Him to answer. It's a "how much more" type of argument: If their sleepy friend was willing to rouse himself at midnight because of their shameless audacity, *how much more* would God do the same? The reason? Simply because He was their *friend!* It was an unorthodox way to make a point. This parable, then, represents Jesus' encouragement to us to keep asking God, keep "knocking on the door" seeking His answers, and keep expecting God to answer our prayers.

THE SNAKE AND THE SCORPION

Immediately following this parable, Jesus gives an illustration of a father and a son (see Luke 11:11-13). He asks the disciples to imagine that the son asks the father for a fish. What will the father do? Will he give his son a snake instead? Or what if he asks for an egg—will the father give him a scorpion? Of course not.

In the same way, Jesus was saying that they could approach God in confidence and make requests, expecting their heavenly Father to answer. It's another "how much more" argument. If the father in the parable gave good gifts to his children, *how much more* would God, who was even better than a good human father, give them gifts? The reason again why God would do this was because they were *in a family relationship with God.* He was their Father, and they were *His children.* Like any good father, He was not going to give them a snake or a scorpion when they asked Him to provide.

Jesus summed up His point by stating, "If you then, though you are evil, know how to give good gifts to your children, how much more will your Father in heaven give the Holy Spirit to those who ask him!" We shouldn't neglect asking God to fill us with His Holy Spirit. It is the best gift of all that God gives to us.

THE UNJUST JUDGE

On a separate occasion, Jesus told His disciples the story of a widow who was seeking justice from the unjust judge. This judge had no desire to grant the widow's request for justice, but because she kept coming back to him and pestering him, he finally relented. Even though he didn't fear God or care what others thought, because she kept bothering him, he decided to give her justice so she wouldn't eventually come back and attack him (see Luke 18:1-5).

In this parable, Jesus again humorously seems to be putting God in the role of the unjust judge. However, as before, that is not the point. Jesus is just making another "how much more" argument. If the unjust judge was willing to give justice because the widow kept bothering him, *how much more* would God give justice to those who keep asking Him? "Will not God bring about justice for his chosen ones, who cry out to him day and night?" (Luke 18:7).

THE PHARISEE AND THE PUBLICAN

Jesus followed up this parable with the story of a Pharisee who went before God and bragged about how wonderful he was and all the good things he had done. Seeing a publican (tax collector) there, he said, "'God, I thank you that I am not like other people—robbers, evildoers, adulterers—or even like this tax collector.'" The publican, however, came humbly before God, beating his chest in remorse for his sins, saying, "God, have mercy on me, a sinner" (Luke 18:9-13).

Jesus' lesson was this: "I tell you that this man, rather than the other, went home justified before God. For all those who exalt themselves will be humbled, and those who humble themselves will be exalted" (Luke 18:14). The starting point for prayer is always relationship, and the starting point for relationship with God is being truthful to Him about who we are and who He is. The publican was starting in the right place.

QUESTIONS FOR PERSONAL APPLICATION AND DISCUSSION

In what way does the topic of prayer plunge us into the mystery of the Trinity? How does the Trinity represent God's intentions for relationships between humans?

_____

_____

_____

_____

_____

Silas Weir Mitchell once said, "He alone has lost the art of living who cannot win new friends." When was the last time you made a new friend? What did you and your friend do to cultivate the friendship?

_____

_____

_____

_____

_____

In what ways did Jesus express to His disciples that He wanted to be their friend? That God the Father wanted to be their friend?

_____

_____

_____

_____

_____

In what ways does Christian faith represent a friendship with Christ? How does prayer play into the equation?

_____
_____
_____
_____

Friendship means developing trust, sharing confidences, and enjoying the same interests as another person. How can you increase your trust in Christ? How can you share your confidences with Christ?

_____
_____
_____
_____

We already know Christ shares our interests. What are Christ's interests? How can we be sure that at least some of our interests match up with His?

_____
_____
_____
_____

What message did Jesus communicate to His critics through the Parable of the Bridegroom about why He and His disciples were not acting the way they thought "religious" people should act? What does this parable (and Jesus' subsequent domestic illustrations) say about prayer and fellowship?

_____
_____
_____
_____

What was Jesus' point about how the disciples should pray in the parables of the Friend at Midnight and the Unjust Judge?

_____
_____
_____
_____

What was Jesus saying to the disciples about how they should approach the throne of God and offer requests in the Parable of the Snake and the Scorpion? What is the greatest gift that God the Father wants to give to us?

_____

_____

_____

_____

_____

What was Jesus teaching through the Parable of the Pharisee and the Publican about humility and relationship with God? In what way did the Publican have the right starting point?

_____

_____

_____

_____

_____

What are some of the reservations and misperceptions about prayer that Jesus addressed through these parables? What are some reservations or misperceptions you have had about prayer?

_____

_____

_____

_____

_____

Note

1. Martyrdom is not just something that happened in ancient Christian history. David Barrett, the world's foremost Christian statistician, estimates that more than 100,000 Christians per year are martyred in countries where the government is hostile to the gospel. Christians under threat of martyrdom know that at any moment they could die. They understand in an experiential way that friendship with Jesus is the essential thing. As Paul wrote, "As long as we are at home in the body we are away from the Lord. For we live by faith, not by sight. We are confident, I say, and would prefer to be away from the body and at home with the Lord" (2 Corinthians 5:6-8).

Source

Henrietta C. Mears, *Highlights of Scripture Part 3: Christ in My Everyday Life and Parables of Jesus, Teacher's Book* (Hollywood, CA: The Gospel Light Press, 1937), pp. 14-21, "Jesus Christ, Our Companion."

THE ART OF STORYTELLING

Jesus' Stand-alone Parables and Parables from the Sermon on the Mount (Matthew 5–7; 12; 19-21; 25; Mark 3; 10; Luke 11–13; 16; 18–19)

SESSION FOCUS

Jesus Christ gives us talents and gifts.

KEY VERSES TO MEMORIZE

Well done, good and faithful servant! You have been faithful with a few things; I will put you in charge of many things. Come and share your master's happiness!
MATTHEW 25:21,23

WEEKLY READING

DAY 1	Matthew 25:14-30; Luke 19:11-27
DAY 2	1 Corinthians 12:1-11
DAY 3	Romans 12:1-21
DAY 4	1 Peter 4:1-11
DAY 5	1 Corinthians 4:1-7; Luke 12:41-48

FOR LEADERS: SESSION AT A GLANCE

SESSION OUTLINE	60 MIN.	90 MIN.	WHAT YOU WILL DO
Getting started	10	15	Pray and worship
Main points of the chapter	25	35	Discuss the parables, focusing on the parable of the talents
Application and discussion	15	25	Discuss personal application questions
Looking ahead	5	5	Prepare for next week
Wrapping up	5	10	Close with prayer or song

Parables from the Sermon on the Mount

Jesus was a master storyteller, and the parables He told touched on all manner of topics. In this session, we will look at the standalone parables that don't fit neatly into the other five categories discussed in these last six sessions of the study. We will begin with a series of parables and illustrations that Jesus told during His Sermon on the Mount in Matthew 5–7.

THE SALT OF THE EARTH

When Jesus saw that crowds of people had gathered to hear Him speak, He went up a mountainside and began to teach. The first story He told after giving the Beatitudes was the Parable of the Salt of the Earth. Jesus said to His followers, "You are the salt of the earth. But if the salt loses its saltiness, how can it be made salty again? It is no longer good for anything, except to be thrown out and trampled underfoot" (Matthew 5:13).

Jesus' listeners were familiar with the image of table salt sprinkled on food to season and preserve it. So part of Jesus' intention here was to indicate that His followers were to become the seasoners and preservers of the earth. Wherever they happened to be sprinkled, they were to bring out flavors of the kingdom of God so that others could "taste and see that the LORD is good; blessed is the one who takes refuge in him" (Psalm 34:8).

Another meaning His hearers would have interpreted from the parable related to the law of Moses. God had told Moses that all grain offerings were to be seasoned with salt. Then God said, "Do not leave the salt of the covenant of your God out of your grain offerings; add salt to all your offerings" (Leviticus 2:13). In addition, the priests' portions of the sacrifices were called a perpetual and "everlasting covenant of salt before the LORD" (Numbers 18:19).

The "covenant of salt" was a reminder to the priests that it was the Lord who provided for their needs through the portions of the sacrifices that were given to support them and their families. This terminology comes up again later in Israel's history when Abijah, ruler of the southern kingdom of Judah, issued a complaint against the northern kingdom, who had rebelled against the rightful successors to the kings David and Solomon. "Don't you know that the LORD, the God of Israel" he said, "has given the kingship of Israel to David and his descendants forever by a covenant of salt?" (2 Chronicles 13:5).

Thus, when Jesus' hearers heard the phrase "salt of the earth," it is likely that they immediately thought of the Lord's provision for the priests through the priestly portion of sacrifices, of acting as priests by bringing others into the presence of the living God, and of being true to God's purposes. Note that Jesus didn't say, "You are the salt of the Church." Jesus wanted His followers to go out into the real world and engage in all sectors of life: the arts, education, commerce, science, law, the service sectors, politics, the professions—everything! He wanted His followers to be an influence on the entire world, not just in their churches and families or among a small circle of religiously minded friends.

LIGHT UNDER A BUSHEL

In this parable, Jesus told His listeners that they were not to be His "secret agent" followers: they were the light of the world and a city on a hill (see Matthew 5:14-16). They were not to take their light and hide it under a "bowl" ("bushel" in the *KJV*). Instead, they were to let their light (good deeds) shine so that others might see them, be drawn to God and glorify the Father.

Obviously, Jesus' point here was not that they were to seek to be "do-gooders" so that they could be better than other people. That would be ridiculous. Rather, Jesus was saying that the way they lived their lives should reflect the light of Christ to the world in a way that others could actually see. Jesus never intended Christian faith to be a strictly private affair, with its members squirreled away in church buildings and committees. It was to be publicly lived, and the values of the Kingdom were to be publicly affirmed.

TREASURES IN HEAVEN

In this parable, Jesus urged His listeners not to put stock in items that are susceptible to thieves, rust, moths, vermin and mold—namely, things that are temporary (see Matthew 6:19-21; Luke 12:33-34). Rather, He told them to store up "treasures in heaven," to invest in things that couldn't be taken away—namely, that which is eternal. When you get right down to it, Jesus wanted them to focus on their relationships with God Himself and with other people—not with material things. This is not to say that material items are bad; they are good gifts from God. The problem comes when people attach too much importance to them.

THE LAMP OF THE BODY

After expounding on prayer, fasting and storing up treasures in heaven, Jesus gave the illustration of "the sound eye" (see Matthew 6:22-23; Luke

11:34-36). "The light of the body is the eye," He said, "if therefore thine eye be single, thy whole body shall be full of light" (*KJV*). Conversely, if one's "eye" is evil, he or she will be full of darkness.

The "eye" is a fascinating term. Of the five senses, the eye is the major gateway to the mind. For this reason, in literature, poetry, philosophy and religion, the eye is often used as a metaphor for physical sensory perception as well as spiritual perception. It can also stand in for the mind (for knowing), for the soul and for the spirit within us. The "eye" filters and colors how we "see" our world—how we understand and process our experiences.

The translation of the word "single" in the *KJV* is also interesting. The Greek term is *haplous*, which has shades of meaning of being simple/single, whole, good in fulfilling its purpose, and sound. English versions of the Bible have translated it as "simple," "single," "sound," "healthy," "unclouded," "good" and "healthy." Putting all these items together, we see that Jesus' point was that the eye was the window to the soul. How we see things reflects the condition of our soul, and the condition of our soul determines what we're going to do with our bodies.

Two Masters

In this one-verse parable, Jesus told His listeners that they couldn't serve two masters—God and money (see Matthew 6:24; Luke 16:13). You may have also heard this stated as "you cannot serve God and Mammon," which is taken from the *King James Version* of Luke's Gospel (Luke 16:13). "Mammon" has come to mean money, wealth, greed and even ill-gotten gains.

Note that there is a difference between wealth and money. Wealth itself is not evil. God gives humans power to create wealth (see Deuteronomy 8:18), and in the Old Testament, it was a gift from God and one of the signs of His *shalom* blessings. Nor is money itself evil; it is merely a means for exchanging goods and services. The problem is in our attitude toward wealth and money (see 1 Timothy 6:10).

There is an ongoing tension in us between the physical and the spiritual, the temporal and the eternal, the realistic and the idealistic, the need for vision and the need to make profits. It's not that we can't be Christians and be involved in business; it's that being involved in business (or any other gainfully employing endeavor) can take our eyes off the prize. Jesus is not saying that we need to choose either God or money! He is saying that we must always keep God first no matter what vocational choices (or financial choices and pressures) we face.

Jesus was not telling us to abdicate responsibility. Elsewhere in Scripture, we are told not to be lazy, not to freeload off of others, to work conscientiously and diligently, to provide for our families, and even to plan for the future (see Luke 14:28-32; 1 Corinthians 4:12; Ephesians 4:28; 1 Thessalonians 4:11). Rather, Jesus was saying that we must keep our worldly affairs in perspective. They do not comprise the whole picture. Of course, this is not always easy to do. It is difficult not to get caught up in greed.

The Camel and the Eye of the Needle

The Parable of the Camel and the Eye of the Needle, not found in the Sermon on the Mount, gives a similar message (see Matthew 19:23-26; Mark 10:23-27; Luke 18:23-27). When a rich man came to Jesus and asked what he must do to obtain eternal life, Jesus told the man, essentially, "You know the commandments, so go do them." The man responded by stating that he had kept them since his youth. Then Jesus told him to sell everything he had and follow Him. The man went away sad, because he had much wealth.

Then Jesus said to His disciples, "Truly I tell you, it is hard for someone who is rich to enter the kingdom of heaven. Again I tell you, it is easier for a camel to go through the eye of a needle than for someone who is rich to enter the kingdom of God." The disciples protested, "Who then can be saved?" Jesus replied, "With man this is impossible, but with God all things are possible." Wealth doesn't get a person into heaven, but it doesn't keep a person out either. Gaining eternal life is impossible based on human effort, but it is possible because God is a God of miracles.

The Birds of the Air and the Lilies of the Field

The parables on money that Jesus told to His listeners provided a direct lead-in to His teachings on how God would provide for their needs. They did not need to have anxieties about our their basic physical needs, because their Father in heaven knew what they needed before they even asked Him.

Jesus told them to consider the birds of the air and the lilies of the field (see Matthew 6:25-34; Luke 12:22-32). Did not God take care of them? Then follows the "how much more" argument: If God took care of them, *how much more* would He take care of them, "O ye of little faith" (*KJV*)?

These parables should hit home for us. We all have concerns about our daily needs and our futures. Jesus is telling us to relax—to seek first God's kingdom purposes and rely on Him to provide all of these things as well. Can we trust Him?

THE PLANK IN YOUR OWN EYE

Jesus then gave two quick parables to warn the people against judging others (see Matthew 7:1-5). The first was an illustration taken from the marketplace: In the same way that they measured out their criticism and condemnation of others, it would be measured to them. The second illustration was drawn from first aid: How could they take a speck out of their neighbor's eye when they had a plank in their own?

In telling these two parables, Jesus was saying that we are often blind to our own faults, so we shouldn't be hypocritical. We shouldn't pretend to help others when we ourselves are ensnared in the same sin. In the same way, we shouldn't deceive ourselves into thinking that we don't need to listen to the criticism of others. We need to listen to what people have to say about us—even if it's exaggerated and overblown—because often there is a grain of truth (or more!) in it to which we need to pay attention.

On the other hand, Jesus' warning against judging doesn't mean that we should never, under any circumstances, judge another person—as we shall soon see.

CASTING PEARLS BEFORE SWINE

Jesus drew on barnyard imagery for His next parable: "Do not give what is holy to dogs, and do not throw your pearls before swine" (Matthew 7:6, *NASB*). This is a warning against doing things such as sharing the gospel with a person who is agitated or who is mocking us. Such a person will just not be receptive to the message, and if we persist in our effort, we will just end up antagonizing them more. We need to graciously move on and wait for a more opportune moment.

THE BROAD AND NARROW WAYS

In this parable, Jesus spoke about two gates and two ways: (1) the wide gate and way that lead to destruction, and (2) the narrow gate and way that lead to eternal life (see Matthew 7:13-14; Luke 13:22-30). Jesus stated that "many" choose the wide way while "few" choose the narrow. This is a pretty scary and straightforward warning to us about not being lackadaisical about which path we choose.

KNOWING A TREE BY ITS FRUIT

Jesus' next parable focused on making accurate judgments about false teachers, whom Jesus effectively calls "wolves in sheep's clothing" (see Matthew 7:15-20). Jesus said, "By their fruit you will recognize them." But wait—what about His previous warning not to judge others (see 7:1-5)? Didn't that mean that we have to accept everyone at all times?

Clearly not. Jesus never asked us to abandon all discernment, logic, common sense and capacity to make wise judgments. Jesus never taught that using those gifts automatically amounted to self-righteous hypocrisy. Rather, those are exactly the kinds of tools that God gives us to exercise faith and reason in the world. It's not a matter of not using them; it's a matter of using them wisely. In this case, Jesus was saying that we need to pay close attention to the character of life produced by the teacher and the teaching. We can't be taken in by a person's charisma or sweet talk.

THE WISE AND FOOLISH BUILDERS

Jesus finished the Sermon on the Mount with the parable of the wise man who built his house upon the rock and the foolish man who built his house upon the sand (see Matthew 7:24-27). Once again, that was imagery to which His listeners would have easily related. They knew that if you built a house upon the sand, when the rains came down, and the streams rose, and the winds blew, that house would collapse. But a house built on a firm foundation—the rock—would stand.

Other Stand-alone Parables

Jesus told a number of other parables throughout the Gospels on various topics. These parables covered issues such as the authority of God, proper uses of wealth, doing the right thing, the gift of salvation, and using one's talents for God.

PLUNDERING THE STRONG MAN'S HOUSE

This parable is contained in all three Synoptic Gospels (see Matthew 12:22-30; Mark 3:22-27; Luke 11:14-23). Prior to telling the parable, Jesus drove a demon out of a mute person, enabling the person to speak. Jesus was able to do this by "the finger of God" (Luke 11:20), indicating that it was a relatively small miracle. (In Deuteronomy 4:34, we read that it took the mighty arm of God to deliver the Israelites from Egypt.)

The crowd was amazed, but some suspected that Jesus was using occult powers. They murmured that He was inspired (or possessed) by a demon—even by Beelzebul (or Beelzebub), who was considered to be the prince of demons (see 2 Kings 1:2-3,6,16). Jesus responded by pointing out the inconsistency of Beelzebul casting out his own demons. Then He gave this parabolic illustration: "How can anyone enter a strong man's house and carry off his possessions unless he first ties up the strong man? Then he can plunder his house."

Beelzebul (Satan) was the strong man, and Beelzebul's "possessions" were the people under his sway. Jesus was saying that God is stronger, and He is in the process of overpowering Satan's house and plundering his possessions. This plundering took place when Jesus and His disciples healed people, cast out demons and preached the gospel.

THE SHREWD MANAGER

This parable told in Luke 16:1-12 is a bit tricky. A manager who worked for a rich man was accused of wrongdoing. The rich man fired him, but before people learned of the firing, the manager went around to the people who owed the rich man money and told them he would help to settle their accounts—at a big discount. The debtors were happy to get the discount, and they were grateful for the manager's role in obtaining it for them. The manager hoped that they would remember they "owed him one" and that he would later be able to collect on that sense of obligation.

When the rich man found out what was happening, he actually *commended* the shrewdness of the dishonest manager! Why? Because the manager had used "worldly wealth" ("unrighteous mammon," *KJV*) to influence people and win friends. Then Jesus told His listeners to take a lesson from the shrewd manager: "I tell you, use worldly wealth to gain friends for yourselves, so that when it is gone, you will be welcomed into eternal dwellings" (16:9). In other words, Jesus was saying that while it was important to be wise about it, it was better for them to use their wealth to gain friends and advance the gospel than it was for them not to use it and thus not advance the gospel.

THE TWO SONS

In this parable, told in Matthew 21:28-32, a man had two sons. The first son said he wouldn't do the father's will, but he had a change of heart and ending up doing it. The second son said he would do the father's will, but he did not do it. From this we see that Jesus isn't looking for people who will just *say* the right things, but for those who will *do* the right things for the Kingdom.

THE WORKERS IN THE VINEYARD

In this parable, a landowner went out early in the morning and hired some day laborers to work in his vineyard (see Matthew 20:1-16). At various times during the day, he went out and hired more men. Finally, about an hour before sundown, he hired some more.

At the end of the day, he paid the men, starting with those most recently hired. He paid everyone the same—a denarius (one day's wages). Understandably, those who worked all day were upset. They complained to the landowner, saying that they worked all day long, including during the hottest part of the day. The landowner replied to one of them, "I am not being unfair to you, friend. Didn't you agree to work for a denarius? . . . Don't I have the right to do what I want with my own money? Or are you envious because I am generous?"

Then, instead of scolding the landowner, Jesus said, "So the last will be first, and the first will be last." This statement forces us to scramble. Isn't Jesus concerned about justice in the fields? In fact, we know that God is very concerned about issues of economic justice—of treating day laborers with decency and respect (see Leviticus 19:13; 25:6,53; Deuteronomy 24:14). Of course, Jesus knew this part of the Mosaic law like the back of His hand.

This story wasn't about justice in the fields. It was about salvation. Jesus was stating that salvation is not something we earn, or get paid for like a wage. It's a free, generous, unearned gift from God. Those who come into the Kingdom late are still welcome. Those who were working in the vineyard early should have considered it a privilege to be working for the Father.

THE PARABLE OF THE TALENTS

This parable, told in Matthew 25:14-30 and Luke 19:11-27, is one of Jesus' most famous. In the parable, a man was preparing to go away on a journey. Before he left, he called his three servants and entrusted his wealth to them, giving a portion to each in proportion to his ability. The first servant received five talents (*NASB*; "bags of gold," *NIV*), the next received two, and the last received one.

The servant who received the five talents immediately went to work and through trade doubled the master's money. The servant with the two talents likewise doubled his portion. But the servant with one talent dug a hole in the ground and hid the master's money there.

After a time, the master returned and settled accounts. To the first two men, he said, "Well done, good and faithful servant! You have been faithful with a few things; I will put you in charge of many things. Come and share your master's happiness!" However, when the last servant returned the one talent back (with a lot of excuses about how fearful he was of the master and how harsh he was), the master said, "You wicked, lazy servant!" He castigated the man for not at least giving the talent to the bankers so he would earn interest on the money.

The master then gave the one talent to the servant with 10 and said, "For whoever has will be given more, and they will have an abundance. Whoever does not have, even what they have will be taken from them." He commanded that the last servant be thrown outside, "into the darkness, where there will be weeping and gnashing of teeth."

God gives each of us talents—natural abilities, spiritual gifts, aptitudes, ambitions, connections, opportunities, resources, inherited wealth, whatever it is—and He expects us to use those gifts for His glory. He expects to "get a return on His investment" in us. We have a choice: We can squander our gifts and refuse to develop ourselves, or we can get busy and try to make the best of what God has given us. In the end, we won't be evaluated on what we don't have; we will be held accountable for how we used what we do have.

Questions for Personal Application and Discussion

As a quick review, briefly state the main point of the following parables that Jesus told during the Sermon on the Mount.

Scripture	Main Point of the Parable
Salt of the Earth (Matthew 5:13)	
Light Under a Bushel (Matthew 5:14-16)	
Treasures in Heaven (Matthew 6:19-21; (Luke 12:33-34)	
The Lamp of the Body (Matthew 6:22-23; Luke 11:34-36)	

SCRIPTURE	MAIN POINT OF THE PARABLE
Two Masters (Matthew 6:24; Luke 16:13)	
Birds of the Air and the Lilies of the Field (Matthew 6:25-34; Luke 12:22-32)	
Plank in Your Eye (Matthew 7:1-5)	
Casting Pearls Before Swine (Matthew 7:6)	
The Broad and Narrow Ways (Matthew 7:13-14; Luke 13:22-30)	
Knowing a Tree by Its Fruit (Matthew 7:15-20)	
The Wise and Foolish Builders (Matthew 7:24-27)	

Now indicate the main point of each of the following stand-alone parables that Jesus told throughout the Gospels.

SCRIPTURE	MAIN POINT OF THE PARABLE
Plundering the Strongman's House (Matthew 12:22-30; Mark 3:22-27; Luke 11:14-23)	
The Shrewd Manager (Luke 16:1-12)	

SCRIPTURE	MAIN POINT OF THE PARABLE
The Camel and the Eye of the Needle (Matthew 19:23-26; Mark 10:23-27; Luke 18:23-27)	
The Two Sons (Matthew 21:28-32)	
The Workers in the Vineyard (Matthew 20:1-16)	
Parable of the Talents (Matthew 25:14-30; Luke 19:11-27)	

What was Jesus saying about how we should use money in the Parable of the Two Masters? How does this relate to His teaching in the parables of the Birds of the Air and the Lilies of the Field? What about in the Parable of the Shrewd Manager?

_____

_____

_____

_____

_____

What was Jesus saying about judging others in the Plank in Your Own Eye and Knowing a Tree by Its Fruit? Should we never judge others? Why or why not?

_____

_____

_____

_____

After telling the Parable of the Two Sons, Jesus told His listeners, "Truly I tell you, the tax collectors and the prostitutes are entering the kingdom of

God ahead of you" (Matthew 21:31). What did He mean by this in terms of what He had just said in the parable?

_____

_____

_____

_____

_____

In the Parable of the Workers in the Vineyard, what was the landowner's rationale for paying every one the same wage? Why did he chide the early workers for complaining? What does this tell us about the kingdom of God?

_____

_____

_____

_____

_____

In the Parable of the Talents, why didn't the master divide the money equally? How did he determine how much each man should have?

_____

_____

_____

_____

The point of this story was not to demean the last servant who had the least ability of the three. What would have been the result if the man with the one talent had done with his gift as the others had done?

_____

_____

_____

_____

In relation to God's kingdom purposes and the gospel, what are you doing with your talents right now?

_____

_____

_____

_____

In 1 Corinthians 4:2, Paul states, "It is required in stewards, that a man be found faithful" (*KJV*). Note that this passage does not say "successful" as the world measures success, but "faithful." How does the world measure success? How is that different from the way God measures success?

_____

_____

_____

_____

Notice that the issue in this parable was not whether the servants had done as much with their talents as others, but whether they had been faithful with what they had been given. What is the difference between the two? What can you do right now to make sure you are being faithful with your gifts?

_____

_____

_____

_____

In Luke's version of this parable, the master was a man of noble birth who went away to be appointed king, though the people didn't want him. What was Jesus saying about the people's expectation of Him as the Messiah?

_____

_____

_____

_____

What additional insights do these details in Luke provide as to the importance of using our talents for God's kingdom?

_____

_____

_____

_____

Source

Henrietta C. Mears, *Highlights of Scripture Part 3: Christ in My Everyday Life and Parables of Jesus, Teacher's Book* (Hollywood, CA: The Gospel Light Press, 1937), pp. 98-105, "Rewards of Faithfulness."

THE URGENCY OF THE HOUR

Jesus' Parables on Life After Death and the End of the Age
(Matthew 21–25; Mark 11–13; Luke 12–14; 16–17; 20–21)

SESSION FOCUS

Jesus Christ is coming again!

KEY VERSE TO MEMORIZE

Truly I tell you, whatever you did for one of the least of these brothers
and sisters of mine, you did for me.
MATTHEW 25:40

WEEKLY READING

DAY 1	Luke 12:16-21; 16:19-31
DAY 2	Matthew 21:18-19; 24:32-36; Mark 11:12-24; 13:28-32; Luke 13:6-9; 21:29-33
DAY 3	Matthew 24:42-51; Mark 13:33-37; Luke 12:39-48
DAY 4	Matthew 25:1-13; Luke 12:35-48
DAY 5	Matthew 25:31-45

FOR LEADERS: SESSION AT A GLANCE

SESSION OUTLINE	60 MIN.	90 MIN.	WHAT YOU WILL DO
Getting started	10	15	Pray and worship
Main points of the chapter	25	35	Discuss following Christ and the urgency of the hour
Application and discussion	15	25	Discuss personal application questions
Looking ahead	5	5	Prepare for next week
Wrapping up	5	10	Close with prayer or song

The Day of Reckoning

We all have witnessed the ferocious suddenness with which everyday life can be violently turned upside down—storms, earthquakes, tsunamis, wildfires, floods, tornados, hurricanes, terrorist attacks, outbreaks of war, the spread of a deadly disease, the crash of a car, plane or a train.

In this session, we will examine parables that are etched with an impending day of reckoning. We all face death, but we know that one day Christ will return to earth. In each case, we don't know when the event will occur; and because of this, we should act as though the time is short. There are pressing and urgent matters to which we need to attend right away—not push off into the indefinite future.

The parables covered in this session are partly about getting into heaven, but that is not the primary focus. Rather, they are about making one's life count for God at the present moment. They are about bearing fruit right now. They anticipate the glorious consummation of all things, when Christ comes again in glory—when, as the Apostle's Creed says, Jesus will come "to judge the quick [those alive when He returns] and the dead."

In this final session, we will review the parables of the Rich Fool (Luke 12:16-21); the Rich Man and Lazarus (Luke 16:19-31); the Wicked Tenants (Matthew 21:33-46; Mark 12:1-12; Luke 20:9-19); the Fig Tree (Matthew 21:18-19; 24:32-36; Mark 11:12-14; 13:28-32; Luke 13:1-9; 21:29-33); the Great Banquet (Matthew 22:1-14; Luke 14:15-24); the Parable of Noah (Matthew 24:37-41; Luke 17:26-36); the Thief in the Night (Matthew 24:42-44; Mark 13:33-37; Luke 12:39-40); A Faithful and Wise Steward (Matthew 24:45-51; Luke 12:41-48); Waiting for the Bridegroom (Matthew 25:1-13; Luke 12:35-48); and the Sheep and the Goats (Matthew 25:31-45).

The Rich Fool

Luke, perhaps a bit more sensitive to issues of wealth and poverty, is the only Gospel writer to include this story. The setting for this parable was Jesus in a question-and-answer session with a crowd of people. Somebody piped up and asked Jesus to tell his brother to share an inheritance with him. Jesus refused to be drawn into the family dispute. "Man," He said, "who appointed me a judge or an arbiter between you?" Turning to the crowd, He said, "Watch out! Be on your guard against all kinds of greed; life does not consist in an abundance of possessions" (Luke 12:13-15). Then He told the following story.

A rich man had some land that was extraordinarily productive. So he decided to tear down his barns and build bigger ones to hold more grain, which was a completely reasonable business decision given the circumstances. But then he said something like this: "Once those barns are built, I will have it made. I'll be able to kick back and eat, drink and be merry." God said to him, "You fool; this night your soul will be required of you" (*NKJV*—in other words, "you will die"). Someone else was going to get to enjoy all those riches. The kicker of the story is this: The same will be true of the selfish person who is not rich toward God.

The Rich Man and Lazarus

This parable that Jesus told, which once again only Luke records, is a story of stark contrasts. A certain rich man liked to parade around in purple (purple was the color of status, wealth and authority) and eat rich food every day. But at his gate, a certain poor man named Lazarus begged for some leftovers. Lazarus was in bad shape. He was covered with sores. The dogs came to lick his wounds.

The time came when Lazarus died, and the angels carried him to heaven (at that time called "Abraham's bosom," because Abraham was the father of Jewish and Christian faith). The rich man also died, but he didn't go to the same place. Instead, he went to Hades, the place where those who are not in Abraham's bosom go to await God's judgment. It was hot there, and the rich man requested some water. Seeing Abraham in heaven, he said, "Father Abraham, have pity on me and send Lazarus to dip the tip of his finger in water and cool my tongue, because I am in agony in this fire."

Abraham denied his request, telling the man that he had lived the good life while he was alive and that he hadn't done anything for others. "Besides," he added, "between us and you a great chasm has been set in place, so that those who want to go from here to you cannot, nor can anyone cross over from there to us." So the rich man asked Abraham to at least send someone to warn his family. Again, Abraham denied this request. "If they do not listen to Moses and the Prophets," he said, "they will not be convinced *even if someone rises from the dead.*"

In this last line, Jesus prefigured His own resurrection. Even though He, the Son of God, had taken on flesh and become a man and would die on the cross and rise again—some would *still* not believe. Why? It was a problem of the heart and soul.

The Wicked Tenants

Matthew's use of parables dealing with the urgency of the hour rises to a crescendo toward the latter part of his book (Matthew 21–25). The first of these stories, the Wicked Tenants, has a sharp edge. In this parable, a landowner planted a vineyard, built a wall, put in a winepress and constructed a watchtower. Then he rented his land out to some tenant farmers and moved to another place. The rental payment was based on shares of the harvest, not on a set amount of rent per month. Normally, the harvest was divided so that the owner received half and the tenant farmers received half.

At harvest time, the landowner sent his servants to collect the rent. But the tenants beat the first man, killed the second, and stoned the third. So the landowner sent his own son, thinking, *Surely they will respect him.* But when the tenants saw him, they said, "This is the heir. . . . Let's kill him, and the inheritance will be ours" (Luke 20:14). So they threw the landowner's son out of the vineyard and killed him. It was a terrible and prophetic indictment.

Let's look at this story more closely. The vineyard represented the people of Israel at that time. The wicked tenants represented those in the religious and political establishment who wanted Jesus dead. Jesus was all but telling His listeners that He was God's Son and they were about to kill Him "in the vineyard" (in Jerusalem), the very heart of the Jewish nation at that time.

Jesus then quoted Psalm 118:22-23 and identified Himself as the stone the builders rejected: "I tell you that the kingdom of God will be taken away from you and given to a people who will produce its fruit," He said. "Anyone who falls on this stone will be broken to pieces; anyone on whom it falls will be crushed" (Matthew 25:43-44). In fact, many Jewish people did end up believing in Jesus, but the nation as a whole did not. The door of salvation to the Gentiles was widening.

The Fig Tree

The Parable of the Fig Tree occurs in all three of the Synoptic Gospels. All three writers include Jesus' immortal line: "Heaven and earth will pass away, but my words will never pass away" (Matthew 24:35; Mark 13:31; Luke 21:33). However, this parable is somewhat hard to understand because today we don't know what to make of Jesus cursing the fig tree so that it dies.

The basic story goes like this: Early one morning as Jesus was on His way to Jerusalem, He was hungry. He saw a fig tree blooming as if it was carrying figs, but on closer inspection, He found that it was barren. Frustrated, Jesus cursed it. Some time passed, and later when Jesus came by that way again, the disciples noticed that the tree had withered. "Look!" Peter said. "The fig tree you cursed has withered!" (Mark 11:21).

Jesus gave them a two-pronged answer as to the meaning of the cursed fig tree. The first prong was that the tree was showing fruit but wasn't bearing fruit, which was the reason why He cursed it. Yet there was more going on than just this one fig tree. This story opens a window on the whole sweep of biblical history.

Like the vineyard in the Parable of the Wicked Tenants, the fig tree represented the nation of Israel. God had invested much in His Chosen People and had high hopes for them, but they had let Him down miserably. Over and over again God had given them the chance to repent and become the kind of people He wanted them to be, and time and again they committed spiritual adultery and turned to other gods. In Scripture, God did not fold His hands and act bored at what His people did. God's emotion to the situation was palpable.

You may recall Hosea is the prophetic book in the Bible in which God told Hosea to marry a prostitute (Gomer). When they had children, God told Hosea to give them prophetic names, including "Not Loved" and "Not My People" (Hosea 1:4-9). This was meant to be a powerful object lesson to bring the Israelites to repentance and act like God's people again. They were actually in danger of going from "chosen people" to "not My people." It was a terrible story, and Jesus' hearers would have been very familiar with it. As God then told the prophet:

> When I found Israel, it was like finding grapes in the desert; when I saw your ancestors, it was like seeing the early fruit on the fig tree. But when they came to Baal Peor, they consecrated themselves to that shameful idol and became as vile as the thing they loved (Hosea 9:10).

Remember that Baal Peor was the place where the Israelites fell into massive spiritual adultery (see Numbers 25:1-3). In cursing the fig tree, then, Jesus was echoing (almost exactly) God's own sentiments expressed through the prophet Hosea. It was a highly symbolic and prophetic statement that raised many of the same spiritual issues that Hosea had raised.

We know that God's purposes do not require any particular people by birth; what God is looking for is individuals from whatever background who will trust Him. As Jesus said, "Therefore I tell you that the kingdom of God will be taken away from you and given to a people who will produce its fruit" (Matthew 21:43).

The second prong of the parable had to do with when Jesus would return to the earth. If you look at a fig tree, you can approximate when it will start bearing fruit, but you can't say when exactly. So it will be with the coming of the Son of Man. No one can say with certainty when it will occur. However, we do know this: Whatever else happens, Christ's words will never pass away (see Matthew 24:35).

The Great Banquet

This parable has a similar theme to that of the Fig Tree. In each case, Jesus' point in telling the parable was to get His listeners (mainly Jewish people) to realize that they were making the wrong choice about His Messiahship.

In this parable, a king prepared a great wedding feast for his son. He sent out invitations weeks in advance and expected everyone to come (he was the king, after all!). On the morning of the feast, the king sent servants out to bid those to come who had been invited. *But they would not come.* They even beat and killed some of the king's messengers. The king was enraged and destroyed their cities.

Jesus' listeners would have known perfectly well what Jesus was saying here. God was preparing a great feast in His kingdom for all those who would come. God had sent His prophets to invite the Pharisees, the rulers and the rest of the Jewish people to come to the feast. But the people had refused to listen and had even killed the prophets (see Matthew 23:31; Luke 11:47). Many of them were on the cusp of refusing to accept the invitation.

The excuses the refusers gave for not attending were pitifully weak: "I have just bought a field, and I must go and see it. . . . I have just bought five yoke of oxen, and I'm on my way to try them out. . . . I just got married, so I can't come" (Luke 14:18-20). So the king sent out a second invitation. This time, he told his servants to bring as many people to the feast as they could, wherever they could find them. These individuals willingly came. They represented the Gentiles, who did not have the advantage of the prophets and the Mosaic law, but who came to Christ anyway.

Jesus ended the parable with a twist. One of the guests came to the feast, but he didn't put on a wedding cloak. In those days, the custom was to provide wedding cloaks for the poorer guests so they could fit in better with the proceedings, but this man had refused to wear it. This was a grave insult to the king and everyone else present. The man thought that his way was just as good as the king's way. But he was wrong, and the king kicked him out of the feast and cast him into the "outer darkness, [where] there shall be weeping and gnashing of teeth" (Matthew 22:13, *KJV*).

The "outer darkness" is a frightening metaphor; the phrase "weeping and gnashing of teeth" speaks of intense, irreparable regret brought upon oneself by a string of bad decisions. It is on the lips of Jesus six times in Matthew (8:12; 13:42; 13:50; 22:13; 24:51; 25:30) and once in Luke (13:28). It is not a situation in which anyone wants to find himself or herself.

The Parable of Noah

Like the other parables in this session, this parable plays on the uncertainty and suddenness with which death (and judgment) can confront us. Jesus gave this parable as part of His response to a question His disciples asked privately: "Tell us . . . what will be the sign of your coming and of the end of the age?" (Matthew 24:3). In other words, the disciples were asking when the end of the world would come.

At this point, we need to consider Jesus' view of history. According to the biblical view, history was moving toward a purposeful end: the consummation of all prophecies and promises that God had made to His people, the putting down of all rebellion against God, the wiping of every tear from our eyes, the elimination of death and sorrow, and the glory of God (see Revelation 21:4). The biblical view of history was not as an endless series of time cycles. In Jesus' parables, this end-time coming of the kingdom of Christ at the end of the world was sometimes in the background and sometimes in the foreground. Scratch beneath the surface and it's always present, which lends a sense of urgency to every parable.

Jesus responded by saying "that day" will be like lightning across the sky—sudden and bright. It will be like a carcass the vultures gather around—something one can't help but notice. It will be as if the natural world is thrown into chaos—the sun darkened, the moon also darkened, the stars falling from the sky, the planets shaken in a cataclysmic event. The Son of Man will appear and the nations will mourn. Angels will accompany a loud trumpet blast and will gather the elect from all over the earth. The sign of the fig tree will appear (see Matthew 24:27-32).

Furthermore, Jesus told His disciples that the hour was near, but that nobody knew when it would happen—not even the Son of Man Himself. It will be like in the days of Noah. Everything seemed normal—the people were "eating, drinking, marrying and giving in marriage." They knew nothing about what would happen, until the floods came and swept them away (see Matthew 24:36-39). Luke adds that it was also the same in the days of Lot—people were eating and drinking, buying and selling, planting and building—until the sulfur rained down from heaven and destroyed them all (see Luke 17:28-29).

The point of all these warnings? "So you also must be ready, because the Son of Man will come at an hour when you do not expect him" (Matthew 24:44).

The Thief in the Night

The Thief in the Night has basically the same message as the Parable of Noah. The thief in the night came secretly, while the people in the home were sleeping. If the owner of the house had known at what hour the thief was coming, he would have kept watch and not allowed the thief to enter. (It's interesting how Jesus describes His coming as a thief in the night—He could find a parable anywhere, it seems!) Mark makes the analogy even clearer by stating that it was the owner of a house who went away and left his servants in charge—they had to do their assigned tasks and keep watch, for they did not know when the master would return. In the same way, Jesus says we need to "keep awake" and stay alert, because we don't know when the Day of the Lord will come, and He will come when we least expect it.

The Faithful and Wise Steward

The parable of the Faithful and Wise Steward played on the same theme as the previous two parables. A steward was like a chef who was hired out to a rich man. He had a group of servants under him, and he was supposed make sure the members of the house were fed on time. He was expected to keep doing that job until the master returned. In this parable, the wise and faithful steward performed his duties. But then Jesus asked His listeners to consider what would have happened if the steward was not wise and faithful, but wicked? The steward figured that since the master was going to be gone a long time, he could abuse the staff and get drunk on the job.

When the master returned, it wouldn't go well with that steward. "He will cut him to pieces and assign him a place with the hypocrites, where there will be weeping and gnashing of teeth" (Matthew 24:51).

Waiting for the Bridegroom

There are actually two "Waiting for the Bridegroom" parables. In Matthew's account, there are 10 young women who were waiting to meet the bridegroom. Five were wise, and five were foolish. The wise ones brought their lamps and oil with them, while the foolish ones brought lamps but no oil. The bridegroom was a long time in coming, and the foolish ones ran out of oil. They went to buy more, but while they were gone, the bridegroom arrived and took the ones who were wise to the wedding banquet.

In Luke's account, there are no virgins. Instead, the parable is about servants waiting for the bridegroom. They keep their lamps burning and are actually ready when he appears. Both parables most likely involve younger adults, and both are encouragements to be watchful and act as if the bridegroom could come at any time. Both the virgins and the servants are waiting for the bridegroom. In both stories the bridegroom takes a long time to arrive, but when he does, it's all of a sudden.

The Sheep and the Goats

The Sheep and the Goats, told only in Matthew's Gospel, is a haunting parable about the last judgment. Jesus said that when the Son of Man comes in His glory, all the nations will be gathered around Him, and He will separate the "sheep" (those who are His) from the "goats" (those who are not with Him). Jesus will invite the sheep into blessed rest, because they acted compassionately toward Him (see Matthew 25:34-36). The sheep, somewhat shocked, will say, "When did we do this?" Jesus will reply, "Truly I tell you, whatever you did for one of the least of these brothers and sisters of mine, you did for me" (25:40).

The reverse will happen with the goats. The Son of Man will tell them to depart, for they did not do His will and act compassionately toward Him. The goats, also shocked, will ask, "When did we . . . not help you?" Jesus will reply, "Truly I tell you, whatever you did not do for one of the least of these, you did not do for me" (25:41-45). When we fail to love and serve others at their point of need, we fail to love the Lord.

It's a sobering parable, to be sure, but it's also an exciting one. When we realize that in serving "the least of these" we are actually serving Christ Himself, it puts a new light on working together to serve our communities in Christ's name.

Questions for Personal Application and Discussion

In the Parable of the Rich Fool, as the name implies, God called the rich man a "fool." In the Bible, a fool can be a smart person—not necessarily someone who doesn't have much going on between the ears. Read Psalms 14 and 53. What is your best guess at what Jesus means here by "fool"?

_____

_____

_____

_____

_____

In the Parable of the Rich Man and Lazarus, what did God require of the rich man (and us), and how did he fail to meet that standard (see Micah 6:8)? In what way is this parable about justice?

_____

_____

_____

_____

_____

In 1 John 2:17, the author states, "The world and its desires pass away, but whoever does the will of God lives forever." How does this relate to the Parable of the Rich Man and Lazarus?

_____

_____

_____

_____

One of Jesus' favorite phrases was, "The last shall be first, and the first last" (Matthew 19:30; 20:8,16; 26:17; 27:64; Mark 9:5; 10:31; 14:12; Luke 13:30). This saying summarizes the great "reversal theme" that we see in the Gospels and in parables such as the Great Banquet. What is that theme? How would this have motivated Jesus' followers to take the gospel to the whole world?

_____

_____

_____

_____

_____

In the Parable of the Wicked Tenants, why did the landowner choose to send his son after the tenants had killed his three servants? How does this parable prefigure Christ's death on the cross?

_____

_____

_____

_____

_____

Read Hosea 1:2-11. What are the three prophetic names God tells Hosea to name his children? Why did God tell Hosea to do this? In cursing the fig tree, how was Jesus echoing these sentiments expressed by God through Hosea?

_____

_____

_____

_____

_____

Notice that it is not all bad news for the nation of Israel. Look again at Hosea 1:7,10-11. What is the tremendous good news for the Jewish people embedded in this passage? How does this relate to what God said to Abraham in Genesis 12:3?

_____

_____

_____

_____

_____

What similarities do you see between the parables of the Wicked Tenants and the Great Banquet? How do both relate to the Israelites' treatment of the prophets and Jesus, the Messiah? What do these parables state will be the result of these actions?

_____

_____

_____

_____

_____

What was the disciples' question that prompted Jesus to tell them the Parable of Noah? Did Jesus answer their question? What does the parable have to say about God's timing?

_____

_____

_____

_____

_____

How does Jesus describe the coming Day of the Lord? How will the events of that day take the people by surprise as the flood did in the days of Noah and the destruction of Sodom and Gomorrah did in the days of Abraham?

_____

_____

_____

_____

_____

What was the main point that Jesus was making in telling the Parable of Noah and the Parable of the Thief in the Night?

_____

_____

_____

_____

In 2 Thessalonians 3:6, Paul told the believers, "We command you, brothers and sisters, to keep away from every believer who is idle and disruptive." What did Jesus have to say about being idle in the parables of the

Faithful and Wise Steward and Waiting for the Bridegroom? What will be the consequences for those who choose not to do the will of God?

_____

_____

_____

_____

_____

As we learned in the Parable of the Talents, God has entrusted us with many good gifts, and He expects us to use those gifts to advance His kingdom. What did Jesus have to say about the importance of using our gifts to serve others in the Parable of the Sheep and the Goats?

_____

_____

_____

_____

_____

Why were both the righteous (the sheep) and the unrighteous (the goats) surprised at Jesus' proclamation of their deeds? How does the attitude of the goats relate to the attitude of the wealthy man in the Parable of the Rich Man and Lazarus?

_____

_____

_____

_____

_____

God wants His people to show compassion on those less fortunate, "the least of these" (Matthew 25:40,45). Is there anyone you know who you think falls into this group? If so, how can you use the talents and gifts that God has given you to help and serve that person?

_____

_____

_____

_____

_____

The Parable of the Sheep and the Goats is actually a profound story on "the hidden Christ," or Christ working behind the scenes through His people to touch the lost and hurting. We are all called to be "sheep" who will go into the world and invite people to the great wedding feast of the Lord Jesus Christ (see Matthew 28:19-20; Revelation 19:7-9). In what ways have you deliberately gone out of your way to find someone to ask to your church or to your Sunday School? How are you sharing the good news of Christ with those in your world?

_____

_____

_____

_____

_____

_____

As you conclude this portion of the study, what are some new insights you have learned about the messages Jesus taught through His parables?

Source

Henrietta C. Mears, *Highlights of Scripture Part 3: Christ in My Everyday Life and Parables of Jesus, Teacher's Book* (Hollywood, CA: The Gospel Light Press, 1937), pp. 73-80, "God's Final Appeal" and pp. 90-97, "The King's Invitation."

LEADER'S TIPS

The following are some general guidelines for leaders to follow when using the *What the Bible Is All About* Bible Studies with a small group. Note that each of the sessions are designed to be used in either 60-minute or 90-minute meetings (see the overview page for a session outline). Generally, the ideal size for group is between 10 to 20 people, which is small enough for meaningful fellowship but large enough for dynamic group interaction. It is typically best to stop opening up the group to members after the second session and invite them to join the next study after the 12 weeks are complete.

GROUP DYNAMICS

Getting a group of people actively involved in discussing issues of the Christian life is highly worthwhile. Not only does group interaction help to create interest, stimulate thinking and encourage effective learning, but it is also vital for building quality relationships within the group. Only as people begin to share their thoughts and feelings will they begin to build bonds of friendship and support.

However, some people resist participating in groups that feature interaction—and with good reason. Discussions can can get off-track, and group members may have opinions and feelings without having any solid knowledge of the topic. Sometimes, members may worry that they will be expected to talk about matters that will make them feel awkward, and some members might be intimidated into silence. Opening up the floor for comments from individuals may result in disagreements being aired, and issues may end up being "resolved" by majority opinion rather than on knowledgeable grounds.

Granted, some people will prefer to bypass any group participation and get right to the content ("I just want to study the Bible—I don't have time to get to know a bunch of strangers"). However, it is never possible to effectively separate knowledge and love. Information without relationship is sterile, and truth apart from touch will turn to untruth. For this reason, while group interaction may at times seem difficult and even non-productive, leaders and group members can work together to achieve positive results.

LEADING THE GROUP

The following tips can be helpful in making group interaction a positive learning opportunity for everyone:

• When a question or comment is raised that is off the subject, either suggest that it be dealt with at another time or ask the group if they would prefer to pursue the new issue at that time.

• When someone talks too much, direct a few questions specifically to other people, making sure not to put any shy people on the spot. Talk privately with the "dominator" and ask for cooperation in helping to draw out the quieter group members.

• When someone does not participate verbally, assign a few questions to be discussed in pairs, trios or other small groups, or distribute paper and pencil and invite people to write their answer to a specific question or two. Then invite several people (including the quiet ones) to read what they wrote.

• If someone asks a question that you don't know how to answer, admit it and move on. If the question calls for insight about personal experience, invite group members to comment. If the question requires specialized knowledge, offer to look for an answer before the next session (make sure to follow up the next session).

• When group members disagree with you or each other, remind them that it is possible to disagree without becoming disagreeable. To help clarify the issues while maintaining a climate of mutual acceptance, encourage those on opposite sides to restate what they have heard the other person(s) saying about the issue. Then invite each side to evaluate how accurately they feel their position was presented. Ask group members to identify as many points as possible related to the topic on which both sides agree, and then lead the group in examining other Scriptures related to the topic, looking for common ground that they can all accept.

• Finally, urge group members to keep an open heart and mind and a willingness to continue loving one another while learning more about the topic at hand.

If the disagreement involves an issue on which your church has stated a position, be sure that stance is clearly and positively presented. This should be done not to squelch dissent but to ensure there is no confusion over where your church stands.

ONE-YEAR BIBLE READING PLAN

✔	BY THE END OF ...	READ THROUGH THESE PASSAGES ...		
		BOOKS OF LAW AND HISTORY	BOOKS OF POETRY AND PROPHECY	NEW TESTAMENT BOOKS
	Month 1	Genesis 1– Genesis 37	Job 1– Job 42	Matthew 1– Matthew 20
	Month 2	Genesis 38– Exodus 25	Psalm 1– Psalm 62	Matthew 21– Mark 8
	Month 3	Exodus 26– Leviticus 23	Psalm 63– Psalm 117	Mark 9– Luke 6
	Month 4	Leviticus 24– Numbers 28	Psalm 118– Proverbs 18	Luke 7– Luke 24
	Month 5	Numbers 29– Deuteronomy 30	Proverbs 19– Isaiah 8	John 1– John 13
	Month 6	Deuteronomy 31– Judges 8	Isaiah 9– Isaiah 43	John 14– Acts 11
	Month 7	Judges 9– 1 Samuel 21	Isaiah 44– Jeremiah 6	Acts 12– Romans 1
	Month 8	1 Samuel 22– 1 Kings 2	Jeremiah 7– Jeremiah 38	Romans 2– 1 Corinthians 11
	Month 9	1 Kings 3– 2 Kings 10	Jeremiah 39– Ezekiel 15	1 Corinthians 12– Ephesians 6
	Month 10	2 Kings 11– 1 Chronicles 17	Ezekiel 16– Ezekiel 45	Philippians 1– Philemon
✔	Month 11	1 Chronicles 18– 2 Chronicles 31	Ezekiel 46– Amos 6	Hebrews 1– 2 Peter 3
	Month 12	2 Chronicles 32– Esther 10	Amos 7– Malachi 4	1 John 1– Revelation 22

TWO-YEAR BIBLE READING PLAN

✔	By the end of . . .	Read Through these Passages . . .		
		Books of Law and History	Books of Poetry and Prophecy	New Testament Books
	Month 1	Genesis 1– Genesis 21	Job 1– Job 20	Matthew 1– Matthew 11
	Month 2	Genesis 32– Genesis 37	Job 21– Job 42	Matthew 12– Matthew 20
	Month 3	Genesis 38– Exodus 6	Psalm 1– Psalm 33	Matthew 21– Matthew 28
	Month 4	Exodus 7– Exodus 25	Psalm 34– Psalm 62	Mark 1– Mark 8
	Month 5	Exodus 26– Leviticus 5	Psalm 63– Psalm 88	Mark 9– Mark 16
	Month 6	Leviticus 6– Leviticus 23	Psalm 89– Psalm 117	Luke 1– Luke 6
	Month 7	Leviticus 24– Numbers 11	Psalm 118– Psalm 150	Luke 7– Luke 13
	Month 8	Numbers 12– Numbers 28	Proverbs 1– Proverbs 18	Luke 14– Luke 24
	Month 9	Numbers 29– Deuteronomy 9	Proverbs 19– Ecclesiastes 7	John 1– John 6
	Month 10	Deuteronomy 10– Deuteronomy 30	Ecclesiastes 8– Isaiah 8	John 7– John 13
	Month 11	Deuteronomy 31– Joshua 14	Isaiah 9– Isaiah 27	John 14– Acts 2
	Month 12	Joshua 15– Judges 8	Isaiah 28– Isaiah 43	Acts 3– Acts 11
	Month 13	Judges 9– 1 Samuel 2	Isaiah 44– Isaiah 59	Acts 12– Acts 20
	Month 14	1 Samuel 3– 1 Samuel 21	Isaiah 60– Jeremiah 6	Acts 21– Acts 28
	Month 15	1 Samuel 22– 2 Samuel 12	Jeremiah 7– Jeremiah 23	Romans 1– Romans 13
	Month 16	2 Samuel 13– 1 Kings 2	Jeremiah 24– Jeremiah 38	Romans 14– 1 Corinthians 11
	Month 17	1 Kings 3– 1 Kings 16	Jeremiah 39– Jeremiah 52	1 Corinthians 12– 2 Corinthians 10
	Month 18	1 Kings 17– 2 Kings 10	Lamentations 1– Ezekiel 15	2 Corinthians 11– Ephesians 6
	Month 19	2 Kings 11– 2 Kings 25	Ezekiel 16– Ezekiel 29	Philippians 1– 1 Thessalonians 5
✔	Month 20	1 Chronicles 1– 1 Chronicles 17	Ezekiel 30– Ezekiel 45	2 Thessalonians 1 Philemon
	Month 21	1 Chronicles 18– 2 Chronicles 8	Ezekiel 46– Daniel 12	Hebrews 1– Hebrews 13
	Month 22	2 Chronicles 9– 2 Chronicles 31	Hosea 1– Amos 6	James 1– 2 Peter 3
	Month 23	2 Chronicles 32– Nehemiah 3	Amos 7– Habakkuk 3	1 John 1– Revelation 9
	Month 24	Nehemiah 4– Esther 10	Zephaniah 1– Malachi 4	Revelation 10– Revelation 22